FREE / STYLE

A Direct Approach to Writing

FREE / STYLE

A Direct Approach to Writing

CHRIS ANDERSON
Oregon State University

HOUGHTON MIFFLIN COMPANY   BOSTON   TORONTO
Dallas   Geneva, Illinois   Palo Alto   Princeton, New Jersey

For my Mom and Dad

Senior Sponsoring Editor: Carolyn Potts
Special Projects Editor: Lynn Walterick
Senior Project Editor: Rosemary Weiss
Senior Production Coordinator: Frances Sharperson
Manufacturing Coordinator: Holly Schuster
Marketing Manager: George Kane

Cover and interior designer: Karen Rappaport

Cover Credit: Painted aluminum mobile, *Essay X,* 1991, by Arthur Bauman, photographed by Jim Scherer

Text credits appear on p. viii

Printed in the U.S.A.

Library of Congress Catalog Card Number: 91-71999

ISBN 0-395-57732-2

BCDEFGHIJ-AM-998765432

CONTENTS

TEXT CREDITS

TO THE READER

I think that we may safely trust a good deal more than we do.

Henry David Thoreau, *Walden*

THIS IS a book to help you write good sentences — sentences that are clear, direct, and natural-sounding. It's a book about the dramatization of self in language, to paraphrase Walker Gibson's definition of style, and the kinds of words and phrases that can help you dramatize a self close to who you really are, in real life, when you're not trying to write papers. And it's a book to help you get those sentences onto the page with less anxiety and frustration, less second-guessing.

Some people believe that writing well depends on secret, complicated codes only insiders know. I don't believe that. Writing is hard work, very hard work. There's no simple formula to make it easy and failsafe every time. But it's also not some arcane mystery for the very educated or the very talented. You can write well, too, right now, building on what you already know, and I try to show how. In fact, I think the first step in writing well is rejecting some of the "rules" and "advice" you think you have to follow and just getting down to it. The subtleties can come later, once you've said what you have to say, and even then you don't have to twist and bend your own inner rhythms too much. The key is to believe in those rhythms, capture them.

I lay all this out in the first two chapters. The first explains a direct method for quickly getting words on the page and revising them for deadlines. The second sketches out a notion of style to guide the process of composing and revising — a notion of style as "natural" and "simple." These are practical discussions. I've tried to write the first two chapters so that you can read them in one sitting and then apply their advice right away, in a real piece of writing you actually have to hand in at school or work. This is what the "Sketchbook" suggestions at the end of both chapters encourage. Whether you need or want to write an essay, a memo, or a report, by the end of the second chapter you should have a draft of it to work with.

The book becomes more technical in Chapters 3–7, more specific about word choice and the order and rhythm of those words in sentences. I'm trying here to describe practical tricks of the trade, some technology for refining and polishing. The sketchbook assignments in these chapters make suggestions for tightening up, tinkering with, possibly rearranging the parts of earlier drafts. In the last chapter I go further, showing what the "free/style" looks like when it's unleashed and unrestrained, recommending strategies to try out when there aren't the limits of academic or business writing.

The first two chapters, then, are the hub, the other five the spokes, the whole book a wheel — which then turns back to the beginning of the cycle with each new writing.

There aren't any drills and exercises. There aren't any hard and fast rules, except when it comes to some matters of proofreading and punctuation. What there is is encouragement, the removing of some silly obstacles, the challenging of some real ones, and some specific, practical tips.

"Style" has been my focus throughout, not "invention" (coming up with ideas in the first place) or "disposition" (the form or organization of writing). I have comments to make on these other subjects, but always from the angle of style itself, as it concerns the actual surface features of a written page, the words and sentences there and the attitude and the personality they project. My advice begins once you already have something more or less figured out to say, however much that might change in the writing itself.

It's important to see the limited claims this book is making (and so their real validity). I'm not trying to explain all there is to explain about style. I'm arguing — from my point of view — that one style in particular, one range of styles, is best and most liberating for most people in most situations (even though there are other styles, on other points of the scale, that have their validity, too).

I'm arguing for what I call the "free/style," because it seems to me the most immediate, workable way to help people believe in themselves as writers and so produce good writing.

Peter Elbow has been a major influence on this project, and an encouraging friend. What I've tried to do here is build on his work, extend it more particularly to the realm of style. I've also tried to combine his theories and approaches with those of Francis Christensen, Richard Lanham, Joseph Williams, and others — opposites apparently, but I want to include them all, get them to talk to each other. Underneath has been the pragmatic, holistic approach to style and voice I learned from my former teacher, William Irmscher.

Carl Klaus gave me much-needed advice and perspective along the way. My friend and colleague at Oregon State, Lex Runciman, did an especially thorough and sympathetic reading of an earlier draft of the book.

A number of other colleagues across the country read the manuscript for Houghton Mifflin and provided detailed and generous commentary:

Charles Anderson, University of Arkansas at Little Rock; Wendy Bishop, Florida State University; John Clifford, University of North Carolina; Neil Daniel, Texas Christian University; Robert DiYanni, Pace University (NY); Sheryl I. Fontaine, California State University, Fullerton; Richard H. Haswell, Washington State University; Katherine Heenan, University of Connecticut; Douglas Hesse, Illinois State University; David Klooster, John Carroll University (OH); Suzanne Ramey Legault, Towson State University (MD); Richard Marius, Harvard University; Shirley K Rose, San Diego State University; Scott Russell Sanders, Indiana University; and James Vanden Bosch, Calvin College (MI).

Carolyn Potts and Lynn Walterick of Houghton Mifflin have been fine people to work with. Lynn's imagination and latitude made it possible for me to write the book I wanted to write.

The good nature and powerful writing of many, many students made this book possible, especially those in my advanced composition classes at Oregon State, fall 1989 and fall 1990. Several of these writers have allowed me to quote from their work: Colleen Brown, Scott Clark, Vickie Cochran, Meg Cooke, Teri Custis, Holly Hardin, Roy Howell, Eric Hunter, Colleen Jenks, Marilyn Koenitzer, Cindy Lederer, Anne Meredith-Wolf, Mary Morris, Pat Ness, and Jay Van Hoff. Mark Brunson, a graduate student in the School of Forestry at Oregon State, gave me permission to quote parts of a letter he wrote to me.

Diane Slywczuk, Anterra, Teri Custis, and Jenny Waite-Phillips, the office staff in the English Department at Oregon State, have been pleasant and efficient, as usual.

I want to thank all these people for their encouragement and support, their questions, their time, their good judgment.

Several parts of the book are based on articles I've previously published: parts of Chapter 1 from "The New Journalism and the New Rhetoric: Freewriting as Product," in Pat Belanoff, Peter Elbow, and Sheryl Fontaine, editors, *Nothing Begins with N: New Investigations of Freewriting,* Southern Illinois University Press, 1991: 243-257; parts of

Chapter 7 from "The Dramatization of Thought," *Rhetoric Review* 4 (1985: 34–43); "Pushing the Outside of the Envelope," in my *Style as Argument*, Southern Illinois University Press, 1987: 8–47; and "Teaching Students What Not to Say: Iser, Didion, and the Rhetoric of Gaps," *Journal of Advanced Composition* 7 (1987): 10–22. "On Screens," the collage essay I include in Chapter 7, appears in a slightly different form in *Willow Springs* 29 (January 1992).

And once again Barb and the kids have weathered the storms. They've forgiven my worrying about other things when I was really worried about this, and they let me have the corner bedroom, by the apple tree, for my study. I hope that one day John, Maggie, and Tim will read this book and understand a little better what's been going on with their dad. Barb, you already know.

Chris Anderson
Corvallis, Oregon

1

SAYING WHAT YOU HAVE TO SAY

....

"Say what you have to say, not what you ought."

—Thoreau, *Walden*

A TWO-STEP METHOD
....

*S*ay a professor has assigned a paper or essay and you have a limited amount of time. Or you have a story or poem you want to write. Or there's a report to get out for your boss. You more or less know what you have to say. You have all the information and expertise. You have some kind of outline, even a couple of sentences. But you're stuck. You're pacing around the room and staring at the screen because you're just not sure how it's all supposed to "sound." You're worried that what you're trying to say won't be "official" or "academic" enough, won't sound "right."

Here's my advice:

Step 1: just write.

Just start writing, not letting your pen leave the page or your fingers the keyboard, not stopping to correct for grammar or spelling, not worrying about any of that: whether it's elegant or proper, whether it makes sense. Forget all the rules you half-learned in school or that you think you should know now. You know what you have to say. Say it. You've got most of it in your head. Let it out. If you get stuck for a minute or draw a blank, don't stop. Repeat the last word until you get back on track. Let it fly. Get it all down, as fast and as directly as you can, however rough the language seems at first. Don't stop.

Step 2: revise.

Now think about all the rules. Scroll back to the beginning or print out the hard copy and get to work: cut all the sentences that don't make sense, untangle other sentences you want to save, keep the really good sentences the way they are. Blend and combine and smooth and rearrange. Delete what's not appropriate and what might get you in trouble. Fancy-up the words you need to. Take the "I" out if you have to. But whatever you do at this stage, try to keep the flow and feel and spontaneity of the first stage—the sense of thinking aloud or of conversation, the impression of movement—because it's that movement and even roughness that will finally make your words seem at least honest and sometimes even powerful.

It's simple, finally: forget the rules/apply the rules; blitz it/fix it; get it all out/shape and polish. This is the process my title is trying to indicate, in part. "Free" suggests the need to forget the rules and just go; "style" suggests the need for polish and revision. The slash between the words is important, too, because it implies that these operations are both necessary and exist in a kind of paradoxical tension.

THE PROBLEM WITH ADVICE

*T*here are lots of fine and famous books out there already describing the rules of good style. Though I take issue with some of this advice later, I think that by and large it's good. You *should* use simpler Anglo-Saxon words whenever you can. Sentences *should* have concrete subjects and concrete verbs, and the modifying phrases should trail the main part of those sentences, refining and detailing direct statement. And so on. You've heard many of these suggestions before.

The problem with such maxims is that you have to be an English teacher to understand them. Their complexities require explanation only possible in a classroom, not to mention some teacherly whip-cracking to get through the many exercises. Deeper than that, so much discussion of style *sounds* like the talk of an English teacher—strict, rule-giving, a pronouncement of do's and don'ts—and in my experience the effect of that kind of talk is to discourage many beginning and average writers. The atmosphere is too proper and Spartan. You'd better sit up straight.

The central paradox of writing with style is that it's hard to do if you're trying to sit up straight. It's hard to have style if you're preoccupied with the rules for having style, even if those rules are accurate and good. You get self-conscious under the influence of maxims, so concerned about being clear and elegant that you can't finally get going.

Good style usually begins when you're deep in the act of saying something important to you and you've forgotten all about style and what the form should look like and you're just writing, thinking about your meanings and your feelings, not the polish and propriety of the final product.

Some or even all of these sentences may have to be fixed or abandoned—they almost always are—but somehow to write with style you need to start with this first zero-degree draft and then capture the rush and force of it as you revise.

MORE ON FREEWRITING
....

*F*reewriting is a brainstorming technique made famous by Peter Elbow in two very fine books, *Writing Without Teachers* and *Writing with Power*. It's a language-spinning machine that you can point at lots of different kinds of writing—a kind of spigot you can turn on to tap into some of your ideas and feelings.

If you're sitting at a computer screen with something to say, just start writing. Don't think about how to *introduce* your idea with some snappy opening or what the first point might be and the transition into the second. Don't think too much about the writing at all. Think about the thinking. Just start writing and don't stop for say ten minutes, or until you're done with this little piece. Write at a comfortable pace. Don't go too fast. Freewriting is a little like running, and you'll lose energy if you start out too fast. But don't go too slow, either, or you'll lose the energy of the words tumbling out and the momentum that builds. If you don't know what to say, write, "I don't know what to say," or repeat the last word you wrote ("wrote wrote wrote wrote") until you come up with something to say. The main thing is not to reread what you've written but to plunge ahead. That's surprisingly hard for most of us since we've been trained by years of school to be proper and not make a mess, especially in writing. But resist those impulses. Turn off the light on the screen and even write blind if you have to, just don't worry about grammar and punctuation and eloquence or anything else. Let the words flow out. Don't let your fingers leave the keys. Don't correct.

No one will ever look at this unless you want them to, so be brave. Take advantage. Try to write while ignoring the reader who might eventually get this (though this is finally impossible, it's a good mental exercise). Say what you really think and to hell with the consequences. (You can tone things down later if you have to. You can revise all of this later.) Imagine that the words are transparent, not there at all, and your raw thinking is showing through.

You can do the same thing with handwriting, too, though the experience is different in interesting ways. Don't let your pen leave the page. Keep up the pace.

Freewriting works best for producing an actual draft of something when you've already done some thinking about the subject. You've gotten all your research and material together. You've mulled over your main argument until you have a tentative focus to start with. Outlining is good, as long as you don't feel bound by it. Sketch out some ideas formally or informally, in a notebook or on a napkin or on a walk, and then freewrite each point, forcing yourself to stay on the subject as much as you can. The order will probably change as you go, and you'll probably come up with new ideas you hadn't planned. That's good. You can reorganize the points later, and besides, freewriting sometimes produces more natural transitions, subtler blends and combinations of ideas, than you can sketch out in advance.

If you haven't had time to incubate, or you're confused, or you only have a very vague idea, start freewriting to generate some possibilities. Use the writing to think about what you want to say. See what comes up. Just don't stop writing.

Here's an example of what you might produce this way, an entry from my current freewriting journal about a walk I take near my house. Notice that the sentences are a little jumbled and fragmentary but that they basically make sense:

```
I seem to need to do things over and over again,
repeat myself, circle round and round the same
thing, in order to feel comfortable with it and
with myself in relation to it. Which is a defini-
tion of habits. Of routine. I think I'd rather take
the same trail a hundred times than hike a hundred
trails. This time I found myself seeing things
things things I hadn't seen before in the other
three walks. Was getting general impressions (I
guess)--impressions--better term?--feelings and
atmospheres and the general zones. Now I was re-
solving things. Details resolving themselves. The
picture was focusing, zooming in. No, it was as if
the things in the woods were for a moment in
boldface, or louder, or clearer against the field
of the other green. Ferns--two kinds, one deli-
cate, the other plainer and almost artificial
looking. The spruce--I think--that have been
planted on the clear cut. The honey-suckle--I
think--among the undergrowth. And the vine maples
--are they?--their stems lifting up the broad
leaves (broad leaf maples?) like upturned palms
```

```
and they seem to levitate there, flattened out in
midair, hovering. I noticed it's Adair Village you
can see from the cut through the power lines by the
forestry cabin. I noticed that the forest isn't as
deep as it seems. It's fragile. It's a fringe and
I can see through it really. The heavy wall of
green is dissolving and there are degrees and
layers and shades of green and light shining
through and balder, barer spots than first seemed,
and the bands of trees shallower.
```

I freewrite at my computer, not worrying about spelling (I've corrected the mistakes here) or even about the rhythm of my sentences. I'm trying to record as clearly and immediately as I can what's going through my mind at the moment of the writing. I want the thinking and the writing to be simultaneous. There's a sense in this entry of my thinking aloud about the writing as I write. I try out different versions of phrases and descriptions as I go. I allow myself to comment on what I've just written, question it. I tread water sometimes, simply repeating the last word I wrote.

HOW TO USE FREEWRITING FOR STYLE: WHY IT HELPS

*M*ost beginning and inexperienced writers overtranslate their own original language into some other language they think is more acceptable or formal or proper and in the process lose the force of their own voice. It's as if they have good, clean words inside them, or the potential for good, clean words, but then they panic—this all happens instantaneously, as they write—and instead of saying directly what they think, start trying to fancy it up. They go to a thesaurus. They say "obtain" instead of "get" and "proceed" instead of "go," as if they've gotten all dressed up in a business suit. Instead of saying, "I think we should," they say, "One might imagine the solution could be . . ." or some other language like that. And pretty soon the sentences are vague and lifeless, or even full of grammatical errors and usage problems, because these writers are using a voice they can't control.

But if you're freewriting, you don't have time to go to a thesaurus and look up a substitute for what you really have to say. If you're freewriting—going at a good pace, warmed up and relaxed—you don't have time to think enough about the elegance and sound of your words to start backing into sentences. You tend to use concrete subjects and concrete verbs. You tend to say things more directly. You tend to say what's really on your mind, or start discovering what's really on your mind. The writing sounds more like "you" and makes more sense, even if there are digressions and problems in it that have to be revised.

Freewriting makes a mess, but in that mess is the material you need to make a good paper or memo or report. You need the mess to get the usable material. The point is that you don't know which is the mess and which is the material when you're writing anyway, so let it all out. You're postponing the critic, the censor, entirely so that everything can get on the table. *Then* the critic can get to work, selecting and choosing from what's in front of you.

There's a parable about this process in Matthew. A man sowed good seed in his field and then his enemies came and sowed weeds among the wheat. When the weeds started growing the servants wanted to pull them up then and there, but the householder wisely ordered that the weeds be left until harvest, "lest in gathering the weeds you root up the wheat along with them." The good and the bad sentences, the good and the bad ideas, are so bound up with each other that they can't be separated until they're all written down and available to intuition. You lose the good when you try to weed out the bad too early.

To put it another way, writing well is like all learning, all education. Education depends on *educing,* on bringing out what's inside to begin with—bringing it out and then improving it, clarifying it, adding to it, putting it in broader contexts. But you have to begin with what's there, take what's inside and use it. Otherwise learning is just affectation. It's something you pretend but don't feel or control because it's not connected to who you are or have become.

Central to this process is the paradox of audience. On the one hand audience is everything, structuring all that you say, determining what you leave out and what order you present things in. To be responsible, to belong to communities, you always need to be imagining what the audience wants and needs. And yet on the other hand, the demands of audience can be tyrannizing, especially in the early stages of writing. You can't write well in the beginning, or get the words out, say what you really mean, if you're trying to second-guess what your audience wants. Thinking about audience too much can lead to pandering and tailoring and even to Madison Avenue opinion sampling—to writing simply to please and impress—which is the source of all the things wrong in writing. The irony is that audiences are most moved by writing that doesn't seem to be a deliberate attempt to impress them.

Maybe it's more accurate to say that in freewriting we're not forgetting audience but holding it at bay, bracketing it. Or maybe it's that we temporarily imagine writing to a safer and more enabling audience, some internalized reader that we can do our best work for, someone we feel free to be ourselves around—knowing that later we can make whatever changes we want to make for the more threatening real-life reader. It's like having a late night conversation with an old friend, or a chat over coffee or beer somewhere. It often happens in real life that we're struggling with what to say for an important presentation or a paper and we turn to a friend or spouse and start trying to explain what we mean, what we're trying to get at, and suddenly it all comes tumbling out, in order, clear and usable.

That's the dynamic. Only by giving yourself permission to generate material that isn't going to be usable in the end can you get the usable material. The provisional *is* the usable, far more often than you think.

SOME EXAMPLES

A typical paragraph from an essay written by one of my freshmen:

> This ritual of parading women before a panel of judges helps determine the goals that our culture pursues. If, in fact, an individual is only as valuable as the appeal of her or his appearance, that individual will seek those things that can enhance that appearance. One's outlook then becomes skewed, a self-centered fixation on the cosmetic. This perspective has blossomed (as a weed) into a multi-million dollar industry. One of the most incredible concepts born out of this idea is that of the tanning salon. Here one can lay down good money to change the hue of the skin while fully conscious of the dangers involved and of the price that skin will have to pay further down the road.

There aren't any grammatical problems here. The passage is just boring and tedious, like the whole paper. I sigh as I pick it up: more going-to-college language, more trying-to-sound-like-you're-writing-an-English-paper language. The diction is inflated, the sentence structure unnecessarily indirect and complicated, none of the subjects direct.

In the original freewrite all the ideas are there but the language is much less forced. I get the sense of the writer thinking about his thinking and not about the writing. He's not trying to impress, and that, ironically, is what impresses me:

> Those beautiful women paraded before a panel of judges! What that says about our culture. If you're only as valuable as the appeal of your looks—if you're only valuable if you're beautiful—then no wonder women work so hard with makeup and clothes. And that's what the beauty pageants represent. Everybody's outlook is skewed, self-centered. Fixations on the cosmetic, and then this of course creates a multi-million dollar industry. Or what about the tanning salon? You lay down good money to get a tan, even though doctors are telling you all the time that the tanning machines are bad for you, that you'll get cancer.

The freewriting needs to be revised. Punctuation needs to be worked out, some sentences blended, other deleted. All I want to point out now is that the freewriting is better than the revision—more interesting, more readable—and that the writer has translated this nice directness into a papery, schoolish language no one really likes to read. The original has a voice, an energy, a movement. I'd rather read the freewrite, even though I also know that it's not quite acceptable as finished writing yet.

Or consider these two versions of a paragraph, the first from the paper the writer submitted for the grade and the second from the original ungraded freewriting she used as a base:

Finished:
> She was beautiful. And I watched her. I watched her lean her curvaceous, cheerleader body against her locker, her weight slightly shifted to one delicate foot, as she stared up with her clear, untroubled baby blues into the eyes of her football player boyfriend. Her long blonde hair curved into a perfect crescent moon on her back, catching all the available light and male attention. Did she always wear her cheerleading outfit, skirt hem dancing on the edge of obscenity, and did he always

wear his football jersey, shining with unscored touchdowns? They couldn't have and yet I don't remember ever seeing them any other way.

Freewriting:

I hate being here. I never wanted to move here. My mom and dad divorce, my mom moves to California and I have to go with her. I hate it. I left my boyfriend Dan, someone who loves me and makes me feel special, to come to this hick school.

In McMinnville I was one of the popular kids. I didn't yet cheerlead in ninth grade but my friends did and they were on the homecoming court. My boyfriend was a football player, a good one. He went to the shrine game. People knew who I was, I was included.

Now I eat lunch by myself. I'm never without a book because I'm alone so much. During the 15 minute brunch break, the worst because I won't even have eating lunch to occupy me, I stand by the wall and try not to look alone.

I watch the cheerleader with the long blonde perfectly curved hair. Her boyfriend is a football player. She seems so much a part of the fabric of this life.

I hate her.

I want to be like her.

What does she do, what does she say that gets her her place?

The polished, translated version seems too writerly or papery to me—canned, staged, played for effect, artificial, too smooth. It's "good" writing in the sense that it's syntactically sophisticated, the diction polished. But I get the feeling that the writer is performing for my benefit, striking up the band so that I will notice what a good writer she is. The freewrite is more interesting for me because it doesn't seem directed *to* me. The writer is inside the experience, recreating it as if it is happening now, on the page. The shorter, more emphatic sentences correspond more to the shape of the time and place they describe, are the kind of statements the writer actually would have made at that time and in that place, not the kind she would deliberately put in a paper. The effect is to suggest that she is thinking about the experience, not about the writing, that she isn't worrying about how she sounds, and *that*—again the irony—is what makes the writing itself more powerful and effective for me. Just on the level of sentence structure I find the rougher, less predictable rhythms of the freewriting more pleasing to the ear than the familiar, symmetrical phrasings of the translation.

SOME CLARIFICATIONS
....

*E*ach burst of freewriting isn't mag-
ically natural and authentic. Often what comes up is too unfocused and
rambling to be of any use, just talking to yourself or looking out the
window, a record of the buzzing in your head. When you lower the
barriers, all kinds of convoluted and pompous and ineffective voices can
and do emerge, all the voices you have inside you and that you keep
absorbing from TV and classes and the culture.

If a page or two of freewriting turns out to be awful, throw it
away and go on, glad to get that language out of your system. Think of
the writing as a warm-up for whatever conventional writing you have
to do that day. In fact, it's a mistake to aim for a good or workable
freewrite each time you sit down at the screen. That attitude only
reproduces the kinds of pressures freewriting is trying to subvert, making you second-guess yourself that way.

The effect is cumulative. You have to do freewriting over time to
get the benefits, and you have to be willing to put up with the messiness
of your own thinking along the way. It's only if you keep freewriting
and letting go of what doesn't work, keep freewriting regularly and in
volume, just as a runner keeps running each day until she gets in shape,
that you eventually seem to slip into a groove, some of the time, and
your own natural rhythms and ways of speaking emerge.

''COAPING'' WITH REVISION
....

*W*hen you do build up enough mo-
mentum to start producing some usable freewriting for a particular
assignment, the freewriting itself is almost never enough. The good
material is usually unformed and chaotic, the good language mixed up
with language you can't use.

Free/style is a two-step method, and the second step, the stage of
revising, is just as important as composing spontaneously without worrying about audience. The key is to harness the energy of the first burst
without harnessing it too much, to translate the freewriting into correct
prose without losing its power and movement.

Here's a convenient scheme for that kind of revising. You don't have to follow the steps in order, or at all. "COAPing" is simply a way to remember some of the things you have to do all at once and intuitively as you start working with your first thoughts:

Cut: cut away all the best or most workable sentences, cut out everything else

Order: put these pieces in the best order, decide what your main point is, put in transitions

Add: do any additional writing that's necessary

Polish: make the sentences smooth and readable:
   · Cut: unnecessary words and phrases
   · Clarify: anything that isn't clear
   · Combine: any sentences that lend themselves to combining, for greater variety and flow
   · Correct: typos, spelling, punctuation, grammar

Using this scheme, for example, I've just spent about ten minutes tinkering with my little freewrite about walking in the woods, cutting and pasting, trying to make the language workable—COAPing with it:

I'd rather take the same trail a hundred times than hike a hundred trails. I seem to need to repeat myself, circle round and round the same thing, in order to feel comfortable with it and with myself in relation to it.
This time on the walk I was getting clearer general impressions of the atmospheres and zones. And the details were resolving themselves, the picture focusing, zooming in, as if the things in the woods were for a moment in boldface, or louder, or clearer against the field of the other green. I noticed there are two kinds of ferns, one delicate and the other plainer, almost artificial looking. Spruce have been planted on the clear cut, and there is honeysuckle among the undergrowth. The stems of the maples lift up their broad leaves like upturned palms, seeming to levitate, flattened out

in midair, hovering. It's Adair Village you can
see from the cut through the powerlines by the
forestry cabin.

I noticed that the forest isn't as deep as it
seems. It's fragile. It's a fringe and I can see
through it. The heavy wall of green is dissolving
and there are degrees and layers and shades of
green, and more light shining through the balder,
barer spots than first seemed. The bands of the
trees seem shallower.

The general movement of the freewriting seems workable, and I want
to keep some of the hard stops in the sentences, some of the abruptness:
"boldface, or louder, or clearer"; "plainer, almost artificial looking."

Cut: I've taken out the phrase "do things over and over again"
and the fragments about habits and routine, letting the
phrases about "circling around" and repeating the hike
carry that idea. Some of the thinking aloud of the original
is gone, too—"no, it was as if" and the "I think." I've just
streamlined, keeping the main blocks of phrases and detail.

Order: I've kept the order, with the exception of the first few
sentences. The passage begins now with what was originally the fourth sentence: "I'd rather take the same trail."
Otherwise what I've done is paragraph, indenting to emphasize the natural transitions of the freewrite. The first
move is simply from the general to the particular: taking
the hike in general to this one hike. And then the third
paragraph emphasizes the idea of the forest's fragility,
which is also a move back outward to the more general
impression.

Add: Not much to add here, just a few words here and there as
part of combining and smoothing the sentences.

Polishing: What were fragments in the original are now complete
sentences. "The spruce that have been planted on the clear
cut" is now "Spruce have been planted on the clear cut."

Mostly I've blended sentences and phrases together, taking what were separate and fragmentary in the original and making them into a single sentence:

```
And the details were resolving themselves, the
picture focusing, zooming in, as if the things in
the woods were for a moment in boldface, or louder,
or clearer against the field of the other green.
```

Later I'll explain that this is a "cumulative" sentence, a sentence that begins with a direct subject-verb statement and then trails modifiers, progressively refining or revising that main statement. It's the principal way of creating sentence variety. The longer, more textured sentences earn the shorter, more direct ones: "It's fragile. It's a fringe and I can see through it." The directness and repetition appeal to me rhythmically. They emphasize. But then that phrasing needs to be followed by the longer "the heavy wall of green," or the passage at that point would get choppy.

All this I do by ear, and reasonably quickly. Part of the key to this method of revising is not to get bogged down in particulars or get too picky about phrasing but to stay fairly close to the original freewriting. That's not only faster and more efficient but saves some of the original voice. Don't try to hit a home run, just get on base. (You strike out a lot less that way.)

You could print out hard copy and do this—sometimes it helps to have the whole passage fixed in front of you—or start playing with it on the screen. Word processing makes the cutting and fiddling easier.

PROTESTING THE CLEAR CUT

A more complicated example.

In the last few weeks I've learned that the School of Forestry at my university is going to harvest trees in the research forest behind my house—the forest where I take the walk. It's part of an experiment in "New Forestry" techniques. There will be a clear cut and then two alternatives: a "shelterwood" and a number of smaller, half-acre "patch cuts."

The neighborhood is understandably upset, even though the research project seems worthwhile in itself. What we object to is not being told sooner. In fact, the information was deliberately withheld.

I attended a public meeting, talked with some neighbors, and then decided that I needed to write a letter.

I didn't outline the letter first, although often when I write like this I do. In this case I simply mulled over what I wanted to say, set the alarm early, got up and made a pot of coffee, and freewrote this, concentrating hard on what I had to say:

> I am writing to protext the extremely late notification residents of MacDonald forest area received about the planned clear cutting.
>
> I am writing to object to the way the public has been informed about the planned clar-cutting in McDonald forest.
>
> to object to how the late the public was told about
>
> I am writing both as a faculty member and as someone who a just bought a home adjacent to where the patchcuts are going to take place—someone who might ot have invested all this money had he known about the cuts.
>
> I'm not objecting to the experiement itself but to the way the school of forestry has deliberately withheld information about it.
>
> The experiment may be fine. I'm not sure how I feel about it. On the hand it's good and important to do research on the New Forestry and on the relationship between managed forests and housing developments. That's what OSU's research forest is for—that kind of research. On the other hand I'm uneasy about some of the attitudes that seem to be implicit here. I wonder if the real reason for the clear cutting is not to make money for the forest's endowment. I wonder how good the science is—the absence of a peer review concerns me.
>
> But that's not what I'm objecting to right now. What deeply bothers me is that public wasn't told about this planned cutting until about aweek be-

fore it was actually going to happen. I learned at the public meeting at Peavy Wednesday night that the decision was made Spring of 1989, over a year ago, but we were not informed until just now.

There seem to be two reasons for this, both disturbing. First, I get the impression that the foresters and scientists didn't want the neighborhood to interfere with the project. They know how sensitive these things are gith now anyway, and how sensitive homeowners would be in particular. Second, we are apparently part of the research—part of the research is into how angry and upset people on the 'urban fringe'' will become if logging is done close to them. Informing us too soon would have biased the experiments. We were guinea bits.

Underneath this seems to be a kind of privileging of expertise and authority. The foresters are the experts and we'r ejust unfinfomred and emotional citizens, sor t of isllily or sloopily concenred with the nonmarket value of the forest —things like beauty (they call it veiwshet or short view aesthetic) and hiking and running (recreational access they call it). Underneath is a lack of respect for what we value and what we know.

At the meeting the other night there was an unfortunate tendency to cast the foresters and researchers as forest-raping bad guys, all malevelonce and profit-motive. I dont' think that's fair. Dean Brown and the four scientists and Jeff Garver did a fine, clear, sensitive job of communicating with us. They handled things well in a difficult, emotionally charged situation. But still I sensed—unspoken but there—a kind of steroetyping of us citizens and homeowners as birkenstock environmentalists without any practical sense or genuine knowledge.

We _do_ have a practical stake in all this, and not just as homeowners. ''Viewsheds'' are importnat, ''recreational access'' is important, all this contentingt values are important—just as important as logging. That's part of the point of the study going on, as I understand it.

The forst is a resaevh forest, yes, but it's a researchforest owned and oeprated by a public university—supported by all of us, for all of us, just as the university is. And those trees are part of our whole enironment, part of the city and the community and our whole viewshed —a part of our lives. A nuclear power plant coulnd't conduct experiments on radioation fall-out by exposing the public. There's a similar kind of fallout here, and a simlar kid of symbotic relationship.

I guess I'm saying that the veiwsheds and the recational access are important, too. I'm saying that that forest is ours, all of ours, not just the university's. We should be involved.'

In this day and age. In this time of diminishing resources and terrible stress on the envirnoment, all trees belong to everybody.

Besides, it's just good rhetorica nd public relations to let people know sooner and get them involved. I suspect that if we'd been brought in sooner there woulnd't be all this bad feeling. If the research is good, if the the university is trying to take the welfare of the neighborhood and community into account, why not risk complicating the process byletting us all in on it.?

In the future I plan to be as involved as I can be in the public planning of a managment plan. I urge you to do what you can to bring more faculty and citizens into that process. And I ask that you be more sensitive to the legitimate concerns of the people who use the forest—use our forest.

Next I printed out the hard copy, got another cup of coffee, and started cutting and ordering what I had:

I am ~~writing~~ to protext the ~~extremely late~~ notification residents ~~of MacDonald~~ forest area ~~received~~ about the planned clear cutting.

I am writing ~~to object to the way the public has been informed about~~ the planned clar-cutting in McDonald forest.

to object to how the late the public was told about

I am writing both as a faculty member and as someone who a just bought a home adjacent to where the patchcuts are going to take place—someone who might ot have invested all this money had he known about the cuts.

~~I'm not~~ objecting to the experiement itself ~~but~~ to the way the ~~school of forestry~~ has deliberately ~~withheld~~ information about it.

The experiment may be fine. ~~I'm not sure how I feel about it~~. On the hand it's good and important to do research on the New Forestry and on the relationship between managed forests and housing developments. That's what OSU's research forest is for—that kind of research. On the other hand I'm uneasy about some of the attitudes that seem to be implicit here. I wonder if the real reason for the clear cutting is not to make money for the forest's endowment. I wonder how good the science is—the absence of a peer review concerns me.

stream-line

Move this ¶ ?

But that's not what I'm objecting to right now. What deeply bothers me is that public wasn't told about this planned cutting until about aweek before it was actually going to happen. I learned at the public meeting at Peavy Wednesday night that the decision was made Spring of 1989, over a year ago, but we were not informed until just now.

conden

There seem to be two reasons for this, both disturbing. First, I get the impression that the foresters and scientists didn't want the neighborhood to interfere with the project. They know how sensitive these things are gith now anyway, and how sensitive homeowners would be in particular. Second, we are apparently part of the research——part of the research is into how angry and upset people on the 'urban fringe'' will become if logging is done close to them. Informing us too soon would have biased the experiments. We were guinea bits.

Reword Underneath this seems to be a kind of privileging of expertise and authority. The foresters are the experts and we'r ejust unfinfomred and emotional citizens, sor t of isllily or sloopily concenred with the nonmarket value of the forest——things like beauty (they call it veiwshet or short view aesthetic) and hiking and running (recreational access they call it). ~~Underneath is a lack of respect for what we value and what we know~~.

At the meeting the other night there was an unfortunate tendency to cast the foresters and researchers as forest-raping bad guys, all malevelonce and profit-motive. I dont' think that's fair. Dean Brown and the four scientists and Jeff Garver did a fine, clear, sensitive job of communicating with us. They handled things well in a difficult, emotionally charged situation. ~~But still I sensed——unspoken but there——a kind of stereotyping of us citizens and homeowners as birkenstock environmentalists without any practical sense or genuine knowledge.~~

We **do** have a practical stake in all this, and not just as homeowners. ~~''Viewsheds'' are importnat, ''recreational access'' is important, all this contentingt values are important——just as important as logging. That's part of the point of the study going on, as I understand it~~.

one para- graph The forst is a resaevh forest, yes, but it's a researchforest owned and oeprated by a public *in part* university——supported by all of us, for all of us, just as the university is. And those trees are part of our whole enironment, part of the city and the community and our whole viewshed——a part of our lives. A nuclear power plant couldn't conduct ex-

periments on radioation fallout by exposing the
public. There's a similar kind of fallout here,
and a simlar kid of symbotic relationship.

What I guess I'm saying that the veiwsheds and the
recational access are important, too. I'm saying
that that forest is ours, all of ours, not just the
university's. We should be involved.'

In this day and age. In this time of diminishing
resources and terrible stress on the envirnoment,
all trees belong to everybody. At the neighborhood meeting..

Besides, it's just good rhetorica nd public
relations to let people know sooner and get them
involved. I suspect that if we'd been brought in
sooner there woulnd't be all this bad feeling. If
the research is good, if the the university is
trying to take the welfare of the neighborhood and
community into account, why not risk complicating
the process byletting us all in on it.?

Make into questi

In the future I plan to be as involved as I can
be in the public planning of a managment plan. I
urge you to do what you can to bring more faculty
and citizens into that process. And I ask that you
be more sensitive to the legitimate concerns of
the people who use the forest—use our forest.

One conclusion can be drawn: people do get
mad, and they have a right to.

A few more minutes at the screen and I came up with this distilled
and more polished version:

Dear Sir:

I am writing to object to how late the public was
told about the planned clear-cutting in McDonald
Forest.

I am writing both as a faculty member and as
someone who just bought a home bordering where
some of the ''patch cuts'' are going to take place.

The experiment may be fine. On the one hand it's
good and important to do research on the New Forestry and on the relationship between managed forests and housing developments. That's the kind of

research OSU's research forest is for. On the
other hand I'm uneasy about some of the attitudes
that seem to be implicit here. I wonder if the real
reason for the clear-cutting is to make money for
the School of Forestry's endowment. I wonder how
good the science is.

But that's not what I'm objecting to right now.
What deeply bothers me is that the public wasn't
told about this planned cutting until about a week
before it was actually going to happen, even though
the decision was apparently made in spring of 1989.

There seem to be two reasons for this, both
disturbing. First, I get the impression that the
foresters and scientists simply didn't want the
neighborhood to interfere with the project. They
knew how sensitive these things are right now
anyway, and how sensitive homeowners can be in
particular. Second, we are apparently part of the
research: part of the research is into how angry
and upset people on the ''urban fringe'' get when
logging is done close to them. Informing us too
soon would have biased the experiments. We were
guinea pigs.

There seems to be a kind of privileging of
expertise going on here. The foresters are the
experts and we're just uninformed and emotional
yuppies, sort of sillily or sloppily concerned
with the ''nonmarket value'' of the forest—things
like beauty (they call it the ''viewshed'') and
hiking and running (''recreational access,'' they
call it).

We <u>do</u> have a valid, practical stake in all this,
and not just as homeowners. The forest is a research forest, yes, but it's a research forest
owned and operated by a public university—
supported (in part) by all of us, for all of us,
just as the university is. And those trees are part
of our whole environment, part of the city and the
community and our whole ''viewshed,'' a part of
our lives. A nuclear power plant couldn't conduct

experiments on radiation fallout by exposing the public. There's a similar kind of fallout here, and a similar kind of symbiotic relationship.

What I'm saying is that the viewshed and the recreational access are important, too. I'm saying that the forest is ours, all of ours, not just the university's.

In this time of diminishing resources and terrible stress on the environment, trees belong to everyone.

At the ''neighborhood'' meeting at Peavy the other night there was an unfortunate tendency to cast the foresters and researchers as forest-raping bad guys, all malevolence and profit-motive. I don't think that's a fair stereotype either. Dean Brown and the four scientists handled things well in a difficult, emotionally charged situation. Earlier Jeff Garver, the forest manager, spent over an hour talking with us in our home, and he was clear and sensitive and understanding.

But couldn't these conversations have happened much sooner? Why wasn't the neighborhood meeting in June instead of August? If the research is good, if the university is trying to take the welfare of the neighborhood and community into account, why not risk complicating the process by letting us all in on it? If nothing else it's good public relations.

Apparently OSU now intends to establish a citizens' advisory group to help develop a long-range management plan for McDonald Forest. That's good. I plan to be a part of that. I hope that you will do all you can to bring more faculty and citizens into the process.

In the meantime I ask that you be more sensitive to the legitimate concerns of the people who use the forest—use our forest. It seems to me that one conclusion can already be drawn from the study

```
going on now: people do get mad, and they have a
right to.
   Sincerely,
```

Obviously the main thing I've done is cut much of the thinking aloud and the starting over and the repetition of the original freewriting, like a sculptor chipping away at a block of stone to liberate the form inside. The thinking aloud is part of what the freewriting allows me to do. It allows me to see various versions of sentences side by side and later pick the best. I don't have to slow down and lose my momentum at the point of composition to make that decision.

I had some trouble getting started. The first few sentences seemed stiff and stilted to me and so I cut them later. It's a difficult situation rhetorically and there's already legalistic and clichéd language to fight through. I had to work to be natural.

Once I was underway, the general structure of the letter seemed to fall into place. I considered moving the paragraph "The experiment may be fine" until later because it delays my getting to the main argument, but doing that seemed to spoil the rhythm of the letter. The paragraph makes me appear reasonable early on, not entirely opposed to cutting in the forest, and yet at the same time I can get in a few quick arguments without having to support them.

The second page bogged down. As I played with it I realized that the paragraph about the neighborhood meeting could go later as a lead into my plea for more public involvement. Originally I was thinking here of the problem of stereotypes, but on reflection I realized that that piece works better emphasizing the theme of communication.

I've added the whole last paragraph. It came to me as I was making the final changes on the screen. It emphasizes.

I've done a little sentence combining and streamlining on the sentence level, though not much. And of course I've corrected all the spelling and the typos and the punctuation.

It's not a perfect letter. I've made a number of compromises in the interests of getting it done. It's too long, for one thing. Freewriting usually opens up a stream of words and I can't always bring myself to channel it too much. I don't want to lose the sense of ideas flowing out, moving fairly quickly. No doubt there are many sentences I could polish more, that need more editing and clarification.

There's also much that I don't say directly because I don't quite know how to. Somehow I've managed to write the whole letter without getting into words the urgency and the feeling that prompted it. I have a sense of some unexpressed center.

But the letter has the virtue at least of being done and in the mail. I didn't wait around for days stewing about it and then doing nothing. And my sense is that there's some virtue stylistically in that. The letter—I think—reads as if I didn't spend days and days trying to make it sound official and impressive. There's a roughness or immediacy about it that I think works. I'm just trying to get things said, as directly and up front as I can.

INTUITION AND TUITION

For longer projects you just freewrite and COAP in sections, working from an outline if you want, piecing parts together. Often you only need to freewrite at the beginning of something longer. Once those wheels are greased, those engines running, the writing can proceed as usual, with rereading and revising as you work through the draft.

Freewriting and COAPing are adaptable processes, as useful for business and academic writing as for personal writing. As the book goes on, I'll be including more examples of pieces written and revised this way for various audiences and purposes.

In revising these two freewritings I've used all the techniques that the rest of *Free/Style* is about, done everything all at once without too much explanation. Next I'll talk explicitly about the theory of style that guides me, later I'll describe in detail what I mean by the "cumulative sentence," and so on. The rest of the book, in other words, is technical elaboration, from different perspectives, of ways to COAP with revision. Sometimes the best parts of a finished piece are only possible as a result of this kind of careful, deliberate revision—are crafted, not spontaneous. Some elements of good prose can only be imitated at first, consciously learned and applied.

But it's important as the discussion gets more and more technical not to forget where it started, here with the act of freewriting. No technical term or understanding can take the place of the intuitions freewriting expresses. If you lose sight of that intuitive sense, concentrate solely on all the techniques and devices I'll be describing, you'll start second-guessing yourself again and censoring out the best material, and the whole balling-up dynamic I've been describing will resume.

Ideally, once you get used to these revision strategies, once you get comfortable with them, they'll be inside you and available the next time you freewrite. Ideally it's a cycle, not a linear sequence, and each time you revise or learn something new you'll add a new element to your repertoire that you can draw on naturally as you compose the next piece.

"Intuition must be educated," William Irmscher says. "The more we have experienced, read, and reflected, the more likely we are to have spontaneous and sound intuitions in new situations." Or as Thoreau puts it, "what we do best or most perfectly is what we have most thoroughly learned by the longest practice, and at length it falls from us without our notice, as a leaf from a tree."

EXTERNALIZING THE MESS

*A*t the same time, you can read the rest of the book entirely apart from this chapter, not relying on freewriting to generate words. You can apply the strategies of style I argue for in the next six chapters however you produce prose, whether you prefer to sweat out a last-minute, one-shot draft or meticulously build up an essay sentence by sentence over weeks of musing and work.

Freewriting is a very useful approach for many people in many situations but it doesn't work for everybody or all the time, and there are other good ways of brainstorming and getting words on the page. The goal, as I'll explain in the second chapter, is a "natural," "simple"-sounding product, and there isn't one fail-safe method for achieving that. Sometimes you can only get the appearance of spontaneity through revision after revision. Sometimes freewriting produces stuffiness and stiltedness.

The process of composing is too complicated and mysterious to boil down to any formula. However you go about it, writing is hard, messy work.

That's the final advantage of freewriting. It admits the mess, externalizes it, then tries to capitalize on it. It helps make you aware of the complicated dynamic of critic and creator, inner and outer, spontaneity and discipline that goes on in every act of composing, even if it's only going on inside your head.

✍ Do three or four freewrites of around ten minutes each. If you have a subject in mind, fine, but don't force it. You won't be using any of these. The goal here is simply warming up and getting used to freewriting. Write about the obvious things: what's happened in your day, the things you've seen and felt and thought. You can just describe the room you're writing in, how you feel at that moment, the experience of freewriting. You can babble, free associate, say the first thing that comes to mind.

FIRST PRACTICE PIECE

✍ When you finish warming up, do a short, two-page writing using the freewriting/COAPing method. If you have a small piece due in your office or for school and you feel comfortable enough with freewriting, try producing a draft of it here. But again, don't force that. Think of it just as a practice piece, a safe place to experiment. It can be light or funny.

Have a focus in mind before you start, though feel free to let that shift as the writing develops. Outline first, too, though feel free to deviate from it. It was okay to ramble before, but here try to stay on the subject, even if you feel yourself digressing or you have to tread water for a while.

If you've discovered a theme in the warmups, write about it again here. If you can't think of a topic, here's a possibility:

- Reflect on a time when writing *worked* for you, a time when you were able to use words effectively and powerfully. What does this experience tell you about the nature of the writing process and the qualities of good writing?
- Some questions to consider: Why did you write? Was the writing assigned or did you do it on your own? What form did the writing take—letter, note, poem, story, report? What was the process: how, when, where did you write? Who was your audience? Why do you think this particular piece worked for you? What does "worked" mean? What does "good" mean?

Do a quick revision of the freewriting for now and hold onto the draft. You'll be using it for closer revision in later chapters.

2

THE FREE/STYLE

When I hear the hypercritical quarrelling about grammar and style, the position of the particles, etc. etc., stretching or contracting every speaker to certain rules of theirs—Mr. Webster, perhaps, not having spoken according to Mr. Kirkham's rule—I see that they forget that the first requisite rule is that expression shall be vital and natural, as much as the voice of a brute or an interjection: first of all, mother tongue; and last of all, artificial or father tongue. Essentially your truest poetic sentence is as free and lawless as a lamb's bleat. The grammarian is often one who can neither cry nor laugh, yet thinks that he can express human emotions. So the posture-masters tell you how you shall walk—turning your toes out, perhaps, excessively—but so beautiful walkers are not made.

—Thoreau, *Journals*

No tricks.

—Raymond Carver

*T*he term *free/style* can also repre-
sent the philosophy of style and voice underneath the freewriting and
COAPing in the last chapter. It can describe not just a way of producing words but a standard of style to aim for as you write and
revise:

Free:	free of wordiness and artifice, seemingly natu-ral and unforced, direct, accessible, reflecting your own instinctive habits of thinking and ex-pression
Style:	and yet at the same time controlled, planned, organized, shaped, appropriate for the audi-ence and situation, not off the top of your head, careful, proofread and free of error, no wasted words
The /:	the creative tension between these two quali-ties, their necessary interdependence

I've suggested that you delay or bracket the critic so that the creative
and generative part of you can operate for a while without being shut
down. Here I'm suggesting that you go on to reimagine that critic, see
it as appreciating a very different style. Some of the barriers you bracket
the critic to avoid are not really there. That critic ought not to believe
in them to begin with.

You don't have to be stuffy and formal and themetalkish.

The freer, more natural voice that comes with this recognition
isn't right for every reader and occasion. Like freewriting, it doesn't
account for everything. But like freewriting, what it does account for is
very useful in much of the writing you do day to day.

NATURALNESS AND SIMPLICITY

*T*he simplest way of giving you the
advice I want to give is also the oldest and most conventional.

When you write, be as simple and natural as possible. Or: when you revise your freewriting, keep the sentences that seem the simplest and most natural, and revise the others to make them seem simple and natural.

You've heard advice like this before. If you lined up every writing text or style book ever written, they'd all have something like naturalness and simplicity at their heart, beginning with Aristotle's *Rhetoric* itself, written two thousand years ago:

> Thus we see the necessity of disguising the means we employ, so that we may seem to be speaking, not with artifice, but naturally. Naturalness is persuasive, artifice just the reverse. People grow suspicious of an artificial speaker, and think he has designs upon them. . . . In style, the illusion is successful if we take our individual words from the current stock, and put them together with skill.

Cicero and Quintilian say much the same thing, and the Renaissance theorists, and so on up to today and the standard advice of Strunk and White's *Elements of Style*: "To achieve style, begin by affecting none." Or: "Write in a way that comes easily and naturally to you, using words and phrases that come readily to hand." There must be a deep wisdom here.

Good writing is writing that isn't trying too hard to be good. It's unaffected, not straining after effect. The writer isn't performing and showing off, isn't using someone else's words, isn't using big and fancy words when simpler ones will do. There's still order and control. These words from the "current stock" are "put together with skill." The effect of naturalness is in some sense an "illusion," a "disguise," since it's often the product of revision. It's a stance, a deliberate strategy. But what persuades us—all that these theorists and teachers have been saying for so long—is at least the appearance that the words are not too staged, too conscious, too syrupy.

What's natural for one writer might not be natural for another. Some writers can get away with fanciness and big words, for example, though most of us can't most of the time. Somehow as readers we can sense when the complicated construction or turn of phrase has come readily, was close at hand.

Related advice: never use a thesaurus. It's always the enemy. When you read a student paper the words drawn from the thesaurus always stick out. We stumble on them.

Or there's the frequent suggestion to write like you talk, or to write as if you're having a serious conversation with a close friend. This is finally a distortion. Writing isn't talking. Writing is always more structured than talking, however simple and natural its tone. But the write-like-you-talk maxim is a useful fiction because it helps you understand that writing is more informal and looser than most beginning writers think it is. It's good to approach that hypothetical limit. It allows you to draw on your natural competence.

Simplicity doesn't necessarily follow from naturalness, since for some people—and for all of us some of the time—it's more natural to be complicated. That's often part of the problem. You have to work for simplicity, cutting away at the pompous and garbled sentences that sometimes come most readily at hand. But for most of us the decision to write more conversationally or to use our own vocabulary and constructions leads over time to more direct sentences and simpler word choices. Most of us aren't naturally fancy or pompous. That's part of the logic behind this typical (and good) advice from Jacques Barzun's *Simple and Direct*:

> I want to lay it down as an axiom that the best tone is the tone called plain, unaffected, unadorned. It does not talk down or jazz up; it assumes the equality of all readers likely to approach the given subject; it informs or argues without apologizing for it task; it does not try to dazzle or cajole the indifferent; it takes no posture of coziness or sophistication. It is the most difficult of all tones, and also the most adaptable.

Simplicity is associated with unaffectedness. It leads to direct sentences. It is the result of the writer's decision to try to say what's on his mind rather than assuming postures or trying to dazzle. Related advice: avoid big words, avoid unnecessarily long sentences, avoid foreign phrases, avoid showy metaphors. All that. Simplicity isn't simple minded. It doesn't mean primer-style sentences or elementary vocabulary. What it means is clear and precise sentences, of whatever length necessary. It means words that are understandable and familiar, appropriate if not plain.

VOICE
. . . .

A broader, less prescriptive form of this advice is to write in your own "voice," to write in a "personal" or "genuine voice": as you revise, keep the sentences that ring true, that seem real, that sound somehow like "you." Cut the others.

This doesn't mean measuring an essay against some objective standard for wordiness or economy or simplicity but instead asking yourself how the words *sound*—whether, in context, the language seems to fit, seems to speak from the experience itself.

We all have characteristic patterns of thinking and talking, verbal tics, conceptual preoccupations, favorite images, a spatial orientation. We all have styles of thinking and expression, drawn from our reading and listening and growing up, in part imitations of others, but also uniquely who we are. When our friends hear us on the phone, they know right away who it is. We sound like ourselves. Writing conveys that sense of sound and character, too, though more faintly, through the words themselves, through the diction and sentence structure.

Somehow readers can sense when we're faking it or putting on airs, when we're going against our own grain.

SOME EXAMPLES
. . . .

T he best way to understand what naturalness or authenticity means is to look at actual pieces of writing. Consult your own experience as a reader.

A pair of essays about nature:

(1) Nature has a way of instilling a feeling of serenity and absolute tranquility. When I am at one with nature, my priorities shift from dealing with societies demands to appreciating what God has given me. The warmth of nature fills my body and replaces the cold feeling I get from a fast-paced lifestyle. When this warmth surrounds me, I am able to open myself up to nature and realize some of the important "facts of life" . . .

By the first evening, my priorities began to change. It's so easy for me to become wrapped up in school, work and to put it bluntly myself, that I don't take the time to appreciate nature. And during our week-long stay, I vowed to myself that I should relax and leave my troubles behind. My vow was not hard to keep, as nature and all its beauty has such a soothing effect upon me. Nature is like a natural sedative. The warmth of the sun upon my skin and the clean-fresh air has a way of turning the everyday stresses and priorities into trivial matters. They become such a small part of the "entire picture" . . .

I work, go to school full-time, am a member of a fraternity and several campus organizations and have a "full-time" girlfriend. I'm always on the go and it seems as though I never have the time to slow down. However, when I was camping the aspects of my life that seemed so important weren't anymore (with the exception of my girlfriend). My world slowed down that week as I learned to appreciate the simple things in life that cause such great pleasure and warmth—at no cost!

(2) I was sitting on the bank of the upper Yaquina Bay, waiting for sport fishermen to return to the adjacent dock. I was being paid to identify and measure their fish. This site was in the area where the river is about a hundred yards wide. There is a public boat ramp here, and a gravelled parking lot where eight boat trailers sat, attached to various vehicles: pickup trucks, old and new, a van, an old Rambler, a Chevy Blazer. There was nothing fancy here. This is the only free launch site west of Toledo, and it's well away from the main roads.

It was very quiet that day. Warm, sunny, peaceful. I was watching the salmon jump as they moved upriver to spawn. I never knew where they were going to jump next. I still don't know why they jump at all. I would try to catch them in the act at the instant they emerged from the water, but they were always just a bit away from where my eyes were directed. I tried scanning the river, thinking that maybe my moving eyes would catch them earlier in their jump, but it didn't help. Then I would gaze at a spot, on the chance that one would jumped where I was looking. My eyes were never quick enough to see the entire leap. With a flash of bright gray-silver, the fish would seem to hang there in mid-air for a moment, just long enough for my eyes to focus, then, with a splash, would be gone, its image fixed in my mind like a photograph, but more vivid, sharp, and clear.

A heron flew by, maybe on his way to munch in the shallows of a mudflat. An egret landed and perched on a not-too-distant piling. I don't know why. He just sat there in the sun, surveying things, dressed in his bright white plumage. He could have been a she. I couldn't tell. . . .

I speak of nature as though it was some coherent entity separate from us humans, but that's not quite the way it is. Being close to nature is being close to life. That's what nature really is: life. We are all a part of nature, as much as any owl, or tree, or any other living thing one might care to name. . . .

Being close to nature helps me to keep in mind those things that are really important in life, and how humans fit in with the Grand Scheme of Things. Maybe it's just a way of keeping my own ego in check, so that I can remember that I am not the most important life-form on Earth. Maybe it's just an escape from inner tensions so that I relax a while, and then, refreshed, rejoin the rest of human society. But for whatever reasons, watching nature, and being part of nature, can help teach us how to live our own lives, if only we have the will to learn.

The first paper could have been written without the writer's actually going camping. There's no evidence that he ever pitched a tent anywhere—no bugs, no rocks under the sleeping bag, no rain. And no place names, no particulars. No evidence of effort or struggle. It's all too easy—"no cost," as he puts it. Boy is citified—boy goes camping—boy is converted to the simple life—everything is fine. A sitcom plot. He seems to have made the whole thing up out of thin air, tacking the little stereotypes together. Priorities shift, priorities change, the air is clean and fresh, nature is a sedative, we should be thankful for What God Has Given Us. I'm not challenging the feelings underneath the words but the words themselves. There's nothing clean or fresh about the phrase "clean-fresh air." There's no evidence of priorities changing in the word "priorities." The writer's use of quotation marks to set off many phrases indicates that he, too, realizes he's walked right out of a greeting card.

The second writer writes about the same theme, but in a radically different and more believable way. His language isn't conversational or colloquial exactly, though it tends in that direction. It's been carefully thought out, each word chosen for reasons. There's been cutting and deliberation. Yet, as the writer says of the dock, "there's nothing fancy here." The diction is simple—few abstractions or grand phrases until the end—and the sentences depend on subject-verb structure followed by modifiers.

The writing is concrete, describing a real event, a particular place and time. It's the Yaquina bay dock, not just any dock. It's a Chevy Blazer, not just a truck (though the writer also uses the unfortunate word "vehicle"). The action unfolds slowly and in a narrow space. This isn't "nature" as in the whole globe or the whole forest or the whole ocean but the nature of a salmon jumping on this particular water, a heron flying by in this particular sky.

I'm moved, too, by the writer's tentativeness and humility. He's not tentative in the sense that he hasn't thought through what he wants to say. He just doesn't try to force answers or solutions. He doesn't quite know where the salmon will jump next or why the egret flies by. It just happens and he records it. Though he talks about the "Grand Scheme of Things," in the end he qualifies it with a "maybe," and his point is that we need to keep ourselves in perspective, scaling ourselves down to size in the face of nature's greatness. The writing does that, too, it seems to me, so the lesson-for-living is earned and believable. We accept it.

One question to ask of writing like this, or any writing, is whether you would keep on reading after the first paragraph if you didn't have to. Ask this even for textbooks or other things you do have to read. Is there anything in the writing that makes you want to keep going, or do you have to fight to maintain interest? Imagine a real-life reading scenario, in other words. In real life we don't have to read most of the things we pick up, and so we don't. What makes us keep reading the things we don't throw back on the pile?

Ask yourself what you really think of a piece of writing, not what you think you should think. That is, some writing is "good" in the sense of organized and clear and sophisticated, but you just fight it for whatever reason. You don't really like it. Admit that feeling and try to figure out where it comes from. Some writing isn't good in these ways—it's sloppy or imprecise—but you can find yourself liking it anyway. That's important. Given that you're making a real effort, that you're in good faith, the key is what's really going on in your mind as you read. Are you bored, angry, involved, resisting, enthused? What? Do your responses vary, go up and down? Can you graph them? Are you more interested at certain spots than at others? Why?

This is a free/reading technique, a postponing of your reading critique for a while to see what your first, untutored responses really are.

By asking these questions, you'll end up confirming experientially much of the advice about naturalness and authenticity. But this way, too, you don't have to commit yourself to some supposedly transcendent set of stylistic values. The questions describe a process, not a dogma, and the answers to them will vary each time, be negotiated by groups and communities of readers, change as you change and as your purpose or audience changes.

Asking these questions of many different examples will also give you a sense of what to look for as you read your own writing. You ask them of yourself: Would I keep reading my own work after the first paragraph if I didn't have to?

A BRIEF LOOK AT PROSE STYLE

*A*nother way to understand what makes writing good is to look at a tradition of writing carried on by some of the most important writers in literature. If these famous and important writers write "simply" and "naturally," why shouldn't we?

When you read the important nonfiction of our tradition, what you discover is that a good number of the rules or restraints you thought you had to deal with aren't really there. Accomplished, professional writers break a lot of those rules. They resist prescriptions, resist the rules invented by the teachers and the language puritans, and instead make an entirely different set of demands. It's bracing, surprising.

The best writers give you permission to write freely and out of your own experience. And they demand that you do. The irony is that the more you read, the more educated you become, the more courage you will have to be simple and natural and yourself.

Montaigne, for example, the sixteenth-century French writer, father of the "essay" form: "The speech I love is a simple, natural speech, the same on paper as in the mouth; a speech succulent and sinewy, brief and compressed; not so much dainty and well-combed as vehement and brusque, rather difficult than boring, remote from affectation, irregular, disconnected and bold; each bit making a body in itself; not pedantic, not monkish, not lawyer-like but rather soldierly." Writing in the midst of religious wars and political conflict, convinced that no rational system of thought could come up with definitive answers to life's big questions, Montaigne invented an open-ended, tentative, personal form of discourse very different from the formalized oratorical writing of his day.

Or Thoreau. The epigraphs to these first two chapters express Thoreau's demand for truth-telling in writing, his insistence on plain, hard seeing. His theories of style reflect his sense of the world. All styles reflect philosophies. That's why they're important. For Thoreau the most important thing was to live "simply," free of material burdens and unnecessary distractions, in touch with the basic and natural. For him style had to be "simple," too, in all the complicated senses of that term:

> A writer who does not speak out of a full experience uses torpid words, wooden or lifeless words, such words as "humanitary," which have a paralysis in their tails.
> The youth gets together his materials to build a bridge to the moon, or perchance a palace or temple on the earth, and at length the middle-aged man concludes to build a wood-shed with them. (*Journals*)

I can't give you a background in reading, of course. All I can do is emphasize how important it is. There is no substitute for reading and reading and reading: George Orwell, E. B. White, James Baldwin, Wendell Berry, Loren Eiseley, Annie Dillard, Gretel Ehrlich, Stephen Jay Gould, Edward Hoagland, Barry Lopez, John McPhee, Scott Sanders, Alice Walker, Tom Wolfe. At the end of this chapter I'm including essays by two of our best contemporary writers as touchstone examples, representative illustrations: "On Going Home," by Joan Didion, and "The Tucson Zoo," by Lewis Thomas. Here are the wonderfully clear, short sentences: "I was flattened" and "I was transfixed" for Thomas; "I am home for my daughter's first birthday" and "Days pass. I see no one" for Didion. Here is the sense of immediacy and presence, the thought seeming to take place in the now of the essay, before our eyes. Here are real people in real places and times sharing the process of their thinking.

"On Going Home" and "The Tucson Zoo" are not the mechanical and formulaic writing so many inexperienced writers think they have to imitate. They're sophisticated and complex—"stylized," in a sense—but they're also intimate and colloquial, made to seem spontaneous. In their basic pattern and movement, in their general tone, they seem close to the way the mind naturally works.

We'll keep coming back to these two pieces in the next few chapters, looking now from this angle, now from that, analyzing their styles and structures in more and more detail. The qualities of language they reveal apply not just to the personal essay but to many different kinds of writing for many different purposes.

THE "STYLE" IN FREE/STYLE
....

I have been emphasizing the "free" part of free/style, because that has to come first. It has to be the grounding, the logic on which everything else is based, or whatever language follows will end up sounding phony and pretentious. But the "style" part is just as important, the part that includes order and control and craft. It's not either freedom or style but both equally—words drawn from the "current stock" but "put together with skill."

Editing for spelling, punctuation, and grammatical correctness is important, for example. It's not the only part of the product or even the most important part, but it is important. Writing that's given to readers without care for these amenities is offensive.

There should be pleasure in writing, too, delight in the sound of words and the deliberate crafting of sentences—"style" in the sense of metaphor, imagery, patterns of sound. The free/style is not the plain style. It doesn't involve counting the number of words and hauling every sentence in front of some sincerity or efficiency meter where its worth is severely tested. It doesn't rule out flourishes and stylistic density, only insist that the fanciness be rooted in the rhythms of thinking and speech. More on this in the next chapter.

And sometimes, of course, you just have to compromise. Sometimes to fit into a situation or show respect for your audience, you have to write more formally or academically than you want to. Free/style doesn't ask you to be impolite or stick your neck out too far. It simply urges you to be as informal and straightforward as you responsibly can be within the limits of the situation.

Effective style depends on a creative tension between freedom and discipline, the simple and the stylish, the writer and the reader. The nineteenth-century English essayist Hazlitt put it this way in a discussion of what he calls the "familiar style":

> It is not easy to write a familiar style. Many people mistake a familiar for a vulgar style, and suppose that to write without affectation is to write at random. On the contrary, there is nothing that requires more precision, and, if I may so say, purity of expression, than the style I am speaking of. It utterly rejects not only all unmeaning pomp, but all low, cant phrases, and loose, unconnected, slipshod allusions. It is not to take the first word that offers, but the best word in common use; it is not to

throw words together in any combinations we please, but to follow and avail ourselves of the true idiom of the language. To write a genuine familiar or truly English style, is to write as anyone would speak in common conversation, who had thorough command and choice of words, or who could discourse with ease, force, and perspicuity, setting aside all pedantic and oratorical flourishes.

The classical theorists called this "artful artlessness."

PLAYFULNESS AND ACCIDENT

*I*n the same way, one of the potential problems with the advice to be simple and natural—ironically—is that it can make you too self-conscious to have fun in your writing. You can become so worried about whether a word or phrase passes the test of the free/style that you tighten up, overtranslating all over again.

The "free" in free/style can also stand for freedom and playfulness. Sometimes it's good to imitate the stuffy and sweet styles deliberately, pull out all the stops and exaggerate those voices and any voices. Experiment. See all the different spins you can give a word or phrase, how silly you can sound, how dour. Sometimes these exaggerations turn out to be successful and you need to keep them. You're hamming it up or gesturing theatrically and suddenly that phrase works. Great. Keep it.

Sometimes there are interesting accidents in freewriting—odd juxtapositions, curious rhythms and orders, a metaphor you hadn't planned—and these work, have an energy or interest. Exploit the accidents. Take advantage of the natural playfulness, even the unruliness, of language.

FINAL LAYERS

*M*any writers are intensely sincere, mean every word they write on the page, but still write wooden and phony-sounding prose. They aren't faking it or trying to be stuffy. Often they're not aware that their prose is clichéd, stilted, affected. Or sometimes they are aware of the gap between their words and their intentions, but they don't know how to bridge it. It's hard to put feelings and ideas into words. Language is never under our control—never simply transparent or facile. Experience always exceeds it. Even successful and famous writers have to struggle to get little pieces of experience into words, and they never fully succeed.

It's also possible for a writer to seem sincere, seem honest, and be faking it every step of the way. The ancients even had specific strategies speakers could use to *appear* trustworthy and sincere and honest—deliberately stuttering or making mistakes, for example, to imply commonness and lack of polish.

The key relationship is as much between the writing and the reader as between the writing and the writer. When a group of readers looks at four or five papers, the question is what passages *seem* to be more authentic or natural or believable. The question is what works. The distinction is between the person and the persona. All we have are the words on the page, the image created by those words, whatever its relationship to the person who wrote them. All we have is the persona—or the mask—of language. Voice is the personality of the persona; an authentic voice, an authentic persona.

What's authentic, furthermore, depends on audience and situation. Sometimes ceremony is authentic and real, because appropriate; sometimes love poetry is. What's authentic or natural for a white male from Oregon isn't authentic for a young woman from Beijing or a priest from Guatemala. Authenticity is culturally determined, not inscribed in nature. We have more than one authentic voice ourselves, can be whimsical or indignant or passionate by turns, all authentically. "Anyone who observes carefully can hardly find himself twice in the same state," Montaigne says. "I give my soul now one face, now another, according to which direction I turn in. . . . All contradictions may be found in me by some twist and in some fashion." Our opinions about what we read change, too, as we read and learn more. We might find something moving in the morning over coffee and then later that evening, sipping wine, wonder what all the fuss was about.

The qualities of the free/style are vague, fluid, floating. There aren't clear edges and finally it's more precise to say that. It's more precise because it's true. It's also more practical for writers because it enables them to use what really works in their writing, not just what passes some external test.

As Thomas observes of the wondrous chemistry of the body, "it's no good standing on dignity in a situation like this, and better not to try. It's a mystery."

MOTHER TONGUE

$\mathcal{Y}$et despite the layers and the fuzziness, readers usually recognize authenticity when they see it. Some words just stand out, ring true.

Here's a final piece of writing, both a good summary of the ideas in this chapter and a fine example of the free/style in academic prose. The student freewrote the first draft in class in about twenty minutes, then revised at home using COAP:

> For Thoreau, style is genuine; it is sincere, it is gut-level writing.
>
> Clear and simple, style is still unique for every individual because we have individual experiences, perceptions. It is being as close to your first thoughts as possible, as close to your first feelings as possible. "They are now allied to life, and are seen by the reader not to be too far-fetched."
>
> "First of all, mother tongue." Mother tongue: the language that we speak with the mother, that which is concerned with sensation, not with ideals. Style is less an activity of the mind than of the body—to tell in concrete terms what your five senses experienced: eyes saw, nose smelled, muscles felt, fingers touched, ears felt/heard, tongue tasted. Human emotions cannot be expressed grammatically, logically; they cannot be adequately expressed in words. Only when we try to paint a word picture do words dance, does the reader begin to understand an emotion. If I read how your heart beat faster, I remember my own heart beating fast—I know how it felt. If your throat tightens up, if your head feels like it's stuffed with cotton, if your eyes are seeing as through a glass jar, I know life seems distant, unreal, translucent.
>
> "Say what you have to say." As in everyday social interaction, you are regarded more highly if you sound sincere, if your words sound like you mean what you say, not what merely sounds good. When I have a thought half-formed and begin to express it, then suddenly realize I might be controversial, I sometimes try to change my sentence in mid-air. This almost always gets me a puzzled, doubtful look: I am not being genuine. I am trying to say what I "ought," not what I "have to say."

Thoreau is saying simply: Readers can tell when a writer is saying what he truly believes, and feels, and when he is merely trying to sound "scholarly." Beauty is always genuine, "as free and lawless as a lamb's bleat."

This passage does all the things that academic writing is supposed to do. It states a thesis, right away, up front. It uses quotes from texts, integrating them into the analysis without letting them overwhelm it. It does more than assert; it demonstrates, explaining each of its claims so that as a teacher I know the student really knows what she's talking about. It's a solid, insightful interpretation.

But it's also interesting and engaged, alive. Most of the sentences have concrete subjects and verbs. There are even some short, direct sentences, even some fragments—emphatic, clear. The diction is concrete and vivid. The sentences have an earthiness or tactileness that draws attention to the words, makes us pay attention. Eyes see and muscles feel. Hearts beat faster. A sentence changes in "midair." There's an "I" here: not a subjective, undisciplined "I," rambling and emoting, but a thinking "I," making analogies, trying to ground the analysis in actual experience.

This is the free/style. This is writing that readers believe in.

S KETCHBOOK

✐ As in the last chapter, do three or four ten-minute freewrites about any subject, rambling and exploring, writing about whatever is on your mind, not worrying about the form or the subject or the grammar and punctuation—just warming up.

You may start developing a theme this second go-around, keep coming back to something. Some usable writing may come up here, but it doesn't have to. Just get more experience with freewriting so that you can freewrite and COAP the second practice piece.

SECOND PRACTICE PIECE

✐ Do a second short piece of writing using freewriting and COAP. Again, this can be something from work or school, something you can actually use right away. It can be the second part of what you started in the first practice piece. But sometimes it's easier to get the feel for this process and later apply the stylistic strategies I'll be talking about if you don't get too invested in the writing yet. Just play and tinker. Easy come, easy go at this stage, although you want the semblance of something with a beginning, middle, and end so that you can experiment with form.

As you freewrite and COAP, keep the "free/style" in mind, its permissions and demands. Revise quickly, saving the draft for closer revision later.

If you don't have a subject from your warm-ups or your work, here's another possible topic:

- Reflect on a time when *reading* worked for you, recently or in the past, a time when some piece of writing succeeded in moving or informing you, sticking in your mind. What are the implications of this experience for your understanding of style? What, in this light, makes writing good?
- Some questions to consider: Was this reading assigned or did you do it on your own? What time of day did you do the reading, and where did you do it? What knowledge or background did you bring to the reading? How much did the subject matter have to do with your experience: Did the writing itself have interest to you, or was it transparent, conveying a subject you care about? Or both? Did you read fast or slow? Was the reading easy or hard? What individual words or phrases stood out as you read? How would you describe the voice of the writer? Do you read on your own, for pleasure, or do you have to force yourself to read? How does your experience as a reader affect your own writing?

....

ON GOING HOME

Joan Didion

I am home for my daughter's first birthday. By "home" I do not mean the house in Los Angeles where my husband and I and the baby live, but the place where my family is, in the Central Valley of California. It is a vital although troublesome distinction. My husband likes my family but is uneasy in their house, because once there I fall into their ways, which are difficult, oblique, deliberately inarticulate, not my husband's ways. We live in dusty houses ("D-U-S-T," he once wrote with his finger on surfaces all over the house, but no one noticed it) filled with mementos quite without value to him (what could the Canton dessert plates mean to him? how could he have known about the assay scales, why should he care if he did know?), and we appear to talk exclusively about people we know who have been committed to mental hospitals, about people we know who have been booked on drunk-driving charges, and about property, particularly about property, land, price per acre and C-2 zoning and assessments and freeway access. My brother does not understand my husband's inability to perceive the advantage in the rather common real-estate transaction known as "sale-leaseback," and my husband in turn does not understand why so many of the people he hears about in my father's house have recently been committed to mental hospitals or booked on drunk-driving charges. Nor does he understand that when we talk about sale-leasebacks and right-of-way condemnations we are talking in code about the things we like best, the yellow fields and the cottonwoods and the rivers rising and falling and the mountain roads closing when the heavy snow comes in. We miss each other's points, have another drink and regard the fire. My brother refers to my husband, in his presence, as "Joan's husband." Marriage is the classic betrayal.

Or perhaps it is not any more. Sometimes I think that those of us who are now in our thirties were born into the last generation to carry the burden of "home," to find in family life the source of all tension and drama. I had by all objective accounts a "normal" and a "happy" family situation, and yet I was almost thirty years old before I could talk to my family on the telephone without crying after I had hung up. We did not fight. Nothing was wrong. And yet some nameless anxiety colored the emotional charges between me and the place that I came from. The

43

question of whether or not you could go home again was a very real part of the sentimental and largely literary baggage with which we left home in the fifties; I suspect that it is irrelevant to the children born of the fragmentation after World War II. A few weeks ago in a San Francisco bar I saw a pretty young girl on crystal take off her clothes and dance for the cash prize in an "amateur-topless" contest. There was no particular sense of moment about this, none of the effect of romantic degradation, of "dark journey," for which my generation strived so assiduously. What sense could that girl make of, say, *Long Day's Journey into Night?* Who is beside the point?

That I am trapped in this particular irrelevancy is never more apparent to me than when I am home. Paralyzed by the neurotic lassitude engendered by meeting one's past at every turn, around every corner, inside every cupboard, I go aimlessly from room to room. I decide to meet it head-on and clean out a drawer, and I spread the contents on the bed. A bathing suit I wore the summer I was seventeen. A letter of rejection from *The Nation,* an aerial photograph of the site for a shopping center my father did not build in 1954. Three teacups handpainted with cabbage roses and signed "E.M.," my grandmother's initials. There is no final solution for letters of rejection from *The Nation* and teacups hand-painted in 1900. Nor is there any answer to snapshots of one's grandfather as a young man on skis, surveying around Donner Pass in the year 1910. I smooth out the snapshot and look into his face, and do and do not see my own. I close the drawer, and have another cup of coffee with my mother. We get along very well, veterans of a guerrilla war we never understood.

Days pass. I see no one. I come to dread my husband's evening call, not only because he is full of news of what by now seems to me our remote life in Los Angeles, people he has seen, letters which require attention, but because he asks what I have been doing, suggests uneasily that I get out, drive to San Francisco or Berkeley. Instead I drive across the river to a family graveyard. It has been vandalized since my last visit and the monuments are broken, overturned in the dry grass. Because I once saw a rattlesnake in the grass I stay in the car and listen to a country-and-Western station. Later I drive with my father to a ranch he has in the foothills. The man who runs his cattle on it asks us to the roundup, a week from Sunday, and although I know that I will be in Los Angeles I say, in the oblique way my family talks, that I will come. Once home I mention the broken monuments in the graveyard. My mother shrugs.

I go to visit my great-aunts. A few of them think now that I am my cousin, or their daughter who died young. We recall an anecdote about a relative last seen in 1948, and they ask if I still like living in New York City. I have lived in Los Angeles for three years, but I say that I do. The baby is offered a horehound drop, and I am slipped a dollar bill "to buy a treat." Questions trail off, answers are abandoned, the baby plays with the dust motes in a shaft of afternoon sun.

It is time for the baby's birthday party: a white cake, strawberry-marshmallow ice cream, a bottle of champagne saved from another party. In the evening, after she has gone to sleep, I kneel beside the crib and touch her face, where it is pressed against the slats, with mine. She is an open and trusting child, unprepared for and unaccustomed to the ambushes of family life, and perhaps it is just as well that I can offer her little of that life. I would like to give her more. I would like to promise her that she will grow up with a sense of her cousins and of rivers and of her great-grandmother's teacups, would like to pledge her a picnic on a river with fried chicken and her hair uncombed, would like to give her *home* for her birthday, but we live differently now and I can promise her nothing like that. I give her a xylophone and a sundress from Madeira, and promise to tell her a funny story. ❑

THE TUCSON ZOO

Lewis Thomas

*S*cience gets most of its information by the process of reductionism, exploring the details, then the details of the details, until all the smallest bits of the structure, or the smallest parts of the mechanism, are laid out for counting and scrutiny. Only when this is done can the investigation be extended to encompass the whole organism or the entire system. So we say.

Sometimes it seems that we take a loss, working this way. Much of today's public anxiety about science is the apprehension that we may forever be overlooking the whole by an endless, obsessive preoccupation with the parts. I had a brief, personal experience of this misgiving one afternoon in Tucson, where I had time on my hands and visited the zoo, just outside the city. The designers there have cut a deep pathway between two small artificial ponds, walled by clear glass, so when you stand in the center of the path you can look into the depths of each pool, and at the same time you can regard the surface. In one pool, on the right side of the path, is a family of otters; on the other side, a family of beavers. Within just a few feet from your face, on either side, beavers and otters are at play, underwater and on the surface, swimming toward your face and then away, more filled with life than any creatures I have ever seen before, in all my days. Except for the glass, you could reach across and touch them.

I was transfixed. As I now recall it, there was only one sensation in my head: pure elation mixed with amazement at such perfection. Swept off my feet, I floated from one side to the other, swiveling my brain, staring astounded at the beavers, then at the otters. I could hear shouts across my corpus callosum, from one hemisphere to the other. I remember thinking, with what was left in charge of my consciousness, that I wanted no part of the science of beavers and otters; I wanted never to know how they performed their marvels; I wished for no news about the physiology of their breathing, the coordination of their muscles, their vision, their endocrine systems, their digestive tracts. I hoped never to have to think of them as collections of cells. All I asked for was the full hairy complexity, then in front of my eyes, of whole, intact beavers and otters in motion.

It lasted, I regret to say, for only a few minutes, and then I was back in the late twentieth century, reductionist as ever, wondering about the details by force of habit, but not, this time, the details of otters and beavers. Instead, me. Something worth remembering had happened in my mind, I was certain of that; I would have put it somewhere in the brain stem; maybe this was my limbic system at work. I became a behavioral scientist, an experimental psychologist, an ethologist, and in the instant I lost all the wonder and the sense of being overwhelmed. I was flattened.

But I came away from the zoo with something, a piece of news about myself: I am coded, somehow, for otters and beavers. I exhibit instinctive behavior in their presence, when they are displayed close at hand behind glass, simultaneously below water and at the surface. I have receptors for this display. Beavers and otters possess a "releaser" for me, in the terminology of ethology, and the releasing was my experience. What was released? Behavior. What behavior? Standing, swiveling flabbergasted, feeling exultation and a rush of friendship. I could not, as the result of the transaction, tell you anything more about beavers and otters than you already know. I learned nothing new about them. Only about me, and I suspect also about you, maybe about human beings at large: we are endowed with genes which code out our reaction to beavers and otters, maybe our reaction to each other as well. We are stamped with stereotyped, unalterable patterns of response, ready to be released. And the behavior released in us, by such confrontations, is, essentially, a surprised affection. It is compulsory behavior and we can avoid it only by straining with the full power of our conscious minds, making up conscious excuses all the way. Left to ourselves, mechanistic and autonomic, we hanker for friends.

Everyone says, stay away from ants. They have no lessons for us; they are crazy little instruments, inhuman, incapable of controlling themselves, lacking manners, lacking souls. When they are massed together, all touching, exchanging bits of information held in their jaws like memoranda, they become a single animal. Look out for that. It is a debasement, a loss of individuality, a violation of human nature, an unnatural act.

Sometimes people argue this point of view seriously and with deep thought. Be individuals, solitary and selfish, is the message. Altruism, a jargon word for what used to be called love, is worse than weakness, it is sin, a violation of nature. Be separate. Do not be a social animal. But this is a hard argument to make convincingly when you have to depend on language to make it. You have to print up leaflets or publish books and get them bought and sent around, you have to turn up on television and catch the attention of millions of other human beings all at once, and then you have to say to all of them, all at once, all collected and paying attention: be solitary; do not depend on each other. You can't do this and keep a straight face.

Maybe altruism is our most primitive attribute, out of reach, beyond our control. Or perhaps it is immediately at hand, waiting to be released, disguised now, in our kind of civilization, as affection or friendship or attachment. I don't see why it should be unreasonable for all human beings to have strands of DNA coiled up in chromosomes, coding out instincts for usefulness and helpfulness. Usefulness may turn out to be the hardest test of fitness for survival, more important than aggression, more effective, in the long run, then grabbiness. If this is the sort of information biological science holds for the future, applying to us as well as to ants, then I am all for science.

One thing I'd like to know most of all: when those ants have made the Hill, and are all there, touching and exchanging, and the whole mass begins to behave like a single huge creature, and *thinks*, what on earth is that thought? And while you're at it, I'd like to know a second thing: when it happens, does any single ant know about it? Does his hair stand on end? ❏

3

THE SOUND OF WORDS

The deepening need for words to express our thoughts and feelings . . . makes us listen to words when we hear them, loving them and feeling them, makes us search the sound of them.

—Wallace Stevens, "The Noble Rider
and the Sound of Words"

*T*he last chapter was an overview—free/style as an attitude and philosophy. Here I want to zero in on the issue of diction. It's individual words and phrases that most obviously carry voice and a sense of naturalness. It's on this level that writers actually start making the cuts I've been describing—the "C" in COAPing—streamlining and toning down, beginning the close work of revision.

It's also here that you can best see the difference between the free/style and the plain style. It's a tricky distinction, easy to blur. On the one hand, improving word choice is a matter of economy, or paring words down to make them more efficient, eliminating what's not absolutely needed. On the other hand, improving diction is a matter of appreciating the sound of words, of taking pleasure in their textures and shapes and rhythms.

BOUGHT VERSUS PURCHASED

Here are the answers to the questions you posed in class Tuesday. I hope they are of assistance. I plan to have an open-ended notebook for the most part and will write about many different subjects. At times, though, I will include directed items. One directed item is opening remarks I need to give to a statewide conference in less than two weeks. I purchased a spiral notebook so I can write wherever I am, but I probably will also type some freewriting. After all, I can type faster than I can legibly write.

The syntax of this paragraph is fine, clear and straightforward. There aren't too many words. It's just that several of the words that are here stick out as unnecessarily formal and stiff:

"posed" instead of "asked"

"of assistance" instead of "help"

"items" instead of "things," "themes," "subjects" (?)

"purchased" instead of "bought"

Instead of the common and expected word, Anne has inserted a more bureaucratic and officious one. The effect is off-putting, distancing—

50

maybe deliberately so. This is a first paper. She doesn't know me as a teacher. I don't know her. It's natural to be unnatural, to keep yourself screened and make yourself seem professional and competent and collegiate. It's like walking into a job interview. You want to be business-like, in charge.

But my advice is to say "bought" anyway, every time, to use the first word you think of, the most informal and conversational word you can possibly use in that situation. Most readers in most situations will inevitably sense the disparity between the more formal word and the actual word underneath it. There will usually be some sense of hiding and inflation, and that's not rhetorically effective.

Most of us have had to deal with too many salesmen and advertisers for inflated language to work. We've been pressured to "purchase a home" instead of "buying a house"; to "purchase an automobile" instead of "buying a car." "Purchase" usually carries a higher price tag, and generally we don't quite get what we paid for. We've had to deal with too many officious bureaucrats wasting our time and giving us the runaround. Clerks and public officials who claim to be "of assistance" usually aren't much "help."

The advantage of "bought" over "purchased" is that it goes against that grain. It's a down-to-earth, concrete word. It gives the impression of directness, forthrightness. (Even if that's not true, it's a useful strategy.) And you won't get in trouble for using it. In what rhetorical situation would anyone fail for using "bought" or "help" or "thing"? Would a boss send the memo back? A customer storm out of the store? A professor lower the grade to a "B"? In what real-world writing situations—situations in which readers don't have much time and aren't reading with a red pen—would even stuffy, finicky readers bother to react to "bought"?

Notice the straightforwardness and informality of Thomas's diction: "all my days," "hankering," "keep a straight face," "while you're at it." He doesn't say, "The general consensus is that insects are to be avoided," but "Everyone says, stay away from ants." In the same way Didion doesn't write, "Birthday celebrations required my presence in the domicile of my parents" but "I am home for my daughter's first birthday." There are big words in Didion, too—"particular irrelevancy," "neurotic lassitude"—as there are in Thomas—"obsessive preoccupation," "instinctive behavior"—but each is appropriate and precisely used. And the voice of both essays is determined by the direct, colloquial diction, the big words controlled by the more down-to-earth ones, kept in check by them.

THE ENVIRONMENT OF LANGUAGE

*A*nne works in an office on my campus, and she told me that it's hard to break out of the habits of bureaucratic jargon she learned there. There's a climate of indirection and inflation in that office, as in most offices, that makes it hard for people to say what they mean, even when they try. It's the climate we all live in. Here, for example, is information on health issues:

> Teenagers of the '90s will be the first generation of American youth exposed to heterosexually available AIDS. Unfortunately, a history of changing expert opinion and fear of openly confronting sexual issues have caused people to avoid facing the realities of AIDS and adopting appropriate preventive behavior.
>
> You have now entered the Comprehensive Abstinence Program (CAP) for Alcohol and Drug Abuse. This program will contain all of the relevant components of a human service system within a single facility. . . . The CAP is an intense structural and therapeutic program for detoxified substance abusers whose primary problems relate to chemicals.

A sign on a trail in the forest behind my house announces:

> The Research management request that all individuals recreating in the adjacent area please follow these guidelines. . . . These guidelines should be exercised by all individuals. It is for your own safety.

At an earlier public meeting with neighbors to discuss the cutting planned by the School of Forestry, the air was full of abstract, academic jargon: "harvest units," "stand configurations," the "matrix of a mature forest," "disturbances within mature stands," "scenic attributes," "alternative harvesting systems," "large-scale biodiversity assessment," "productivity enhancement." It's hard to see the forest for the trees when the language is so abstract.

That's part of the point. One of the problems with language like this is that it's euphemistic, a disguising of the unpleasant, as George Orwell argues so passionately in his "Politics and the English Language." Writing in the aftermath of World War II, he describes political speech and writing as "the defense of the indefensible." To disguise the harsh realities of decision making, Orwell says, "political language has to consist largely of euphemism, question-begging, and sheer cloudy vagueness":

> Defenseless villages are bombarded from the air, the inhabitants driven out into the countryside, the cattle machine-gunned, the huts set on fire with incendiary bullets: this is called *pacification*. Millions of peasants are robbed of their farms and sent trudging along the roads with no more than they can carry: this is called *transfer of population* or *rectification of frontiers*. People are imprisoned for years without trial, or shot in the back of the neck or sent to die of scurvy in Arctic lumber camps: this is called *elimination of unreliable elements*. Such phraseology is needed if one wants to name things without calling up mental pictures of them.

The disparity we feel in much of the wordiness around us is between Latinate abstractions and the mental pictures they are abstractions from, the concrete particulars of cattle and farms and people on roads.

The abstractions of forestry and other academic disciplines are usually less sinister, and—as I'll discuss later—not entirely invalid, but they sometimes attempt the same kinds of screens and hedgings. Mark Brunson, a graduate student in forestry, explained how this works in a letter to me, a response to my letter in the local paper protesting the research harvest:

> Now that I spend much of my working life talking with foresters, I find myself increasingly amazed by how euphemistically we speak. Medical terms are popular. When we decide what we want to do with a particular stand of trees, we call it a "prescription." One of the first forest growth models was named "Prognosis." If some natural agent threatens to slow a management goal with a forester has "prescribed" for a particular stand, he or she will probably find the best "treatment" for that stand. Thus, if deciduous bushes are thriving in a recently harvested stand and competing with plantation seedlings, the forester may decide to "treat the hardwoods." The word "treat," of course, is synonym for "kill."

In the same way "research harvest" can be a synonym for "clear-cutting." On the other side of this question, "saving" the "old growth" is in part a euphemism disguising the economic consequences of people out of work and mill towns dying.

Doctors relying on the rhetoric of "prescription" soften the blows of bad news with scientific terminology. Anxious relatives in the waiting room have an impression of ordered, white-coated analysis before the news hits them. In *Illness as Metaphor*, Susan Sontag suggests that there are other motives for such obscurity, too, for the medical profession and for all professions, including the urge for professionalism itself. Complex terminology signals insider status while excluding the uninitiated.

There's just the desire to seem important and powerful, to sound like a doctor or scientist or intellectual. Too many literary critics say "valorize" instead of "value" and "problematize" instead of "complicate." The result is a language most students can't penetrate, a language at odds with the concreteness of the literary language it describes. An example:

> In many fields—literary studies, film history, classics, anthropology, and history of science to name a few—there is a new urgency about the categories through which the body is regarded. Is it primarily a gendered body? A disciplined body? A textualized body? A resisting body? Such questions are being addressed in histories and theories of sexuality, pleasure, and subjectivity that explore the many ways that peoples in different historical periods and cultures have represented, constructed, and regulated the body in transforming it into a human subject. Such transformations typically occur in contexts of subordination and domination rooted in modes of power and authority.

In addition to whatever problems of bad faith and social status there are here, there's also simply the problem of not being able to understand what's being said.

IN DEFENSE OF JARGON

Analysis like the kind I've been making can degenerate into anti-intellectualism, just a knee-jerk reaction to any big words and complicated concepts. We need some abstractions and jargon, too.

One of the advantages of abstract jargon is its power to organize complex information. Often we don't want to get immersed in the welter of detail. We need to synthesize and condense, and abstract jargon terms do that, providing conceptual perspective. Terminology within disciplines and fields can also serve as shorthand for ideas that would take too long to explain each time. People inside the fields know the full definition and so don't need it unpacked. Later in his letter to me, Mark Brunson goes on to defend some of his own jargon in these terms, taking me to task for my criticism of the "aesthetic preference" and "viewshed" jargon I'd heard at the public meeting:

> Some of the terms you mentioned, while they may be jargon, are used because they're more precise. When we met, you referred to yourself as a "rhetorician." For you it's a much more precise term than "English teacher," but it would sound like gobbledygook to someone who doesn't know a rhetorician from a rhesus monkey. When I speak of someone's "aesthetic preference" for a forest, I use the term to refer to a specific facet of someone's perception of the forest environment, which can be distinguished from other perceptual elements such as the forest's perceived suitability for a favorite recreation activity. The word "viewshed," which, I, too, found absurd when I first heard it, serves an equally precise need. A viewshed is that portion of the environment which provides the scenic resources (if you will) available at a particular location, just as a watershed is that portion which provides the water resources which are available. The word may not be found in Webster's, but I believe it has greater utility than many of the words which can be found there.

Within certain communities and disciplines, abstract terms have a great precision. The question is audience. My use of the term "rhetorician" didn't make much sense when I first met Mark because, unlike my colleagues in the English department, he didn't know that that term indicates a kind of training and specialization. The School of Forestry's use of the term "viewshed" didn't make much sense at the first public meeting for exactly the same reasons, not if communication was the goal.

There are good and bad abstractions, good and bad uses of jargon, appropriate and inappropriate situations. What we resist as readers is not the jargon itself but a sense that it's being used to put one over on us—which it very often is. A "gendered body," after all, just refers to sex, male or female. The phrase is finally just a snow job, inadvertent or not, an attempt to obscure and dominate (no doubt rooted in modes of power and authority).

BIRCHES AND BUICKS

*T*he corollary of this is not just using the most familiar word but also the most concrete and specific, the one that gets the closest to real people doing real things in the world. Try to supply, however briefly, the "mental pictures" that Orwell says are hidden behind abstractions. "Tree" and "bush" and "flower" are usually better than "vegetation." "Birch" and "juniper" and "columbine" are better still. "Vehicle" has less interest than "car," and "car" less interest than "Buick." "Weasel" and "field mouse" are superior, just as words, as terms on a page, to "rodent." "Teacher" is superior to "educator," "father" and "mother" to "parent." This works for verbs, too: "shook" is better than "vibrates"; "crashed" better than "impacted."

Sometimes you have to use the vaguer, Latinate terms like "vegetation" or "rodent" because they are more inclusive, more general. But the simpler terms have the advantage of concreteness, of invoking real, particular objects and places and people rather than blurring them in lifeless and potentially misleading, even dishonest terms. They also just *sound* better. They have a texture, a shape—are knotty, slippery, hard, soft, more noticeable *as words*, as objects themselves. Kenneth Burke says that words "glow." They have a resonance of connotation and implicit meaning on the page, some more than others, depending on the context. Concrete words, words of place and landscape and sensory experience, usually glow more than polysyllabic, "-tion" words. We are interested in what we can see and feel.

This is what makes Didion's prose work. Her strategy is to provide the concrete details "coded" in terms like "sale-leaseback" and "right-of-way condemnations": "the yellow fields and the cottonwoods and the rivers rising and falling and the mountain roads closing when the heavy snow comes in." She empties out a drawer and shows us the contents, the inherently interesting "stuff" of her life: "A bathing suit I wore the summer I was seventeen. A letter of rejection from *The Nation*, an aerial photograph of the site for a shopping center my father did not build in 1954. Three teacups handpainted with cabbage roses and signed 'E.M.,' my grandmother's initials."

This doesn't mean being fancy, piling up adjectives and adverbs, giving everything a particular name. Orwell intensifies his language by generally naming: "villages," "huts," "peasants," "farms," "lumber camps"—a hint of a real life somewhere. In the midst of "pacification" and "transfer of population," these basic words of living and working have a kind of humility and honestly that compels us.

ROLLICKING LANGUAGE

Υou can go too far with concreteness, too, indulging in a descriptive inflating just as off-putting as bureaucratic mumbo-jumbo:

> Rollicking music pumped into the air by a carousel organ tempted everyone within earshot to join the circular parade. Glass jewels and sparkling mirrors scattered inviting beams of light into the eyes of the passing throng.

"Passing throng"? You mean "the crowd" or "the people"? "Circular parade"? You mean "merry-go-round"? "Rollicking"? Who in any real-life situation ever uses the word "rollicking"? How would you react if someone came up to you as you were standing in front of a merry-go-round and actually said something like, "Isn't that music being pumped into the air rollicking?" The language here is all writerly, papery, phony, the kind of prose writers use when they're trying to dazzle, impress, inflate. Every noun is modified by an adjective, every simple word replaced by some clichéd, thesaurus phrase. The effect is cloying, sicky sweet. Good writing uses words from the common stock. Good writing works through nouns and verbs, not through adverbs and adjectives.

Notice how Didion's prose works primarily through nouns and verbs and the direct naming of details:

The baby is offered a horehound drop, and I am slipped a dollar bill "to buy a treat." Questions trail off, answers are abandoned, the baby plays with the dust motes in a shaft of afternoon sun.

Versus my revision:

The innocent infant is quietly offered a delicious horehound drop, while I am slipped—surreptitiously, of course—a single crisp dollar bill with which, as they said, "to buy a treat." Irrelevant questions trail off like dying footfalls, the equally irrelevant answers are soon abandoned, my beautiful daughter frolics quietly with the almost invisible dust motes in a single, iridescent shaft of mellow California sun.

The other problem with the carousel paragraph is that it's made up of prepackaged, preowned phrases, phrases that are just out there, ready to be grabbed and used. Crowds are very frequently "passing throngs." Mirrors almost always "sparkle." This is the issue, too, in the first "nature" essay in the last chapter. It seems smoothly written at first, but that's because it's made up of nothing but tag phrases, easy rhythmic fillers: "absolute tranquility," "priorities shift," "warmth of nature," "fast-paced lifestyle," "soothing effect," "clean fresh air," "everyday stresses." The student didn't write this. It wrote him. We've heard these phrases a thousand times before, on car commercials, in travel brochures, in real-estate come-ons. All the writer had to do was put them in the microwave for a couple of minutes and out they came, an instant pastiche suitable for nearly every occasion.

CUTTING: A FIRST CASE

*T*he term "wordiness" is often applied to the inflations we've been talking about. There's just too much word for the particular job required. It's too big and grand, too noticeable. The related problem is having too many words—not just one inflated term but a whole lot of inflated terms—or just a whole lot of terms, inflated or not.

Here's an example of both kinds of wordiness:

I am standing tiptoe on the brink of an MA in English literature, a single foreign language all that is between me and that dubious achievement. Most of the prose writing I do is oriented academically. I have in the past written papers for classes, and enjoyed doing so until an abrupt increase in page requirements (coincidental with the beginning of graduate school) made the writing of a paper a task plagued by terror. I have difficulty writing at a length greater than eight or ten pages. A twenty or thirty page length requirement seems preposterous, impossible, and the fear that I will not be able to meet it impedes my ability to write at all.

And a revision:

I am on the brink of an MA in English, a foreign language the only thing I have left to do. Most of what I write is academic. I have written and enjoyed writing papers for classes until I started graduate school and had to write much longer papers. I was terrified. I have trouble writing anything longer than eight or ten pages—a twenty or thirty page paper seems preposterous, impossible, and I get so worried that I won't be able to do it that I can't write at all.

I've exaggerated the colloquial and down-to-earth in my revision of this student's paragraph, and I've fiddled with the syntax to make it more direct (see Chapter 5). But mainly I've cut and economized: "tiptoe," "oriented," "dubious," "coincidental," "plagued by terror"—all gone.

When you revise, ask yourself: What can I stand to lose? What do I absolutely have to have here to say what I mean? What's extra, repetitive, unnecessary, or digressive? The general rule of thumb: less is more. A maxim: you're not finished revising until you've cut your best sentence. "Murder your darlings," as Bernard DeVoto (and many others) used to tell creative writing students.

THREE MORE CASES

*H*ere's a sample of Anne's freewriting, evocative in its details, but too loose stylistically.

It was definitely an autumn day, in temperament and in color. The sky was gray, an even gray. Every once in a while it would rain. Quietly, not thunderously. This was a day to spend inside, perhaps with a fire going, perhaps warm enough to open the doors and let in the autumn smells. This was definitely not a type of day to have to do anything. No projects or chores should have to be done on a day like this. A day like this should just be enjoyed. Relaxing in the dampened world. Re-creating oneself. Perhaps a walk in the woods. With a poncho on, listening to the rain drops on the hood. Wiping the rain drops from your nose. Wishing you had windshield wipers for your eyes. Walking alone, making rustling sounds, walking quietly, occasionally hearing a bird here, an animals' movement over there. Hearing the sound of rain in the tree canopy. Smelling. Really smelling the wet vegetation. There's something powerful about that smell. You never smell it in the city, walking around the blocks. Only when you get into a forest path.

Revision:

It was an autumn day, in temperament, in color. The sky was gray, an even gray. Once in a while it would rain. Quietly, not thunderously. This was a day to spend inside, perhaps with a fire going, perhaps warm enough to open the doors and let in the autumn smells. This was not a day to do anything. No projects or chores. A day like this should just be enjoyed. Relaxing in the dampened world. Re-creating oneself. Perhaps a walk in the wood. With a poncho on, listening to the rain on the hood. Wiping the drops from your nose. Wishing you had windshield wipers for eyes. Walking alone, making rustling sounds, walking quietly, hearing a bird here, an animal over there. Hearing the sound of rain in the tree canopy. Smelling. Really smelling the wet. There's something about that smell. You never smell it in the city, walking around the blocks. Only when you get into a forest path.

I've cut out adjectives and adverbs as much as possible ("definitely," "occasionally") to let the direct statements speak for themselves, register more directly. Eliminating the "and" between "temperament" and "color" creates a sense of pleasing abruptness. I've taken out unnecessary exposition by cutting the phrase "should have to be done on a day like this." It's a clunking phrase, it seems to me, and the fragment "no projects and chores" gets the job done anyway. "Animal's movement" is a smaller example. "Movement" is a weak word, implied in context.

Eliminating "vegetation" and "powerful" goes a little further, slightly changing the meaning of the phrases, making them less specific and more evocative.

The effect of the revision is to reveal the evocativeness underneath the extra verbiage of Anne's original—one of her first sketchbook entries after the "purchased" paragraph. The principle is to eliminate anything that doesn't work and see how whatever is left blends together.

This passage comes from Roy's sketchbook.

During the night our refrigerator stopped working. Not without warning exactly. The last time this happened, several months ago, I gave it a sharp jolt with the side of my fist, gaining its cooperation so that it started running again, like nothing had happened. I started to believe that nothing had, and thought that it might be OK. Well, it's not. It's six A.M., the refrigerator is off, the freezer full of food is defrosting, and it is a problem that will have to wait until this afternoon.

At first I felt a moment of panic, with the thought of fifty dollars of food being consumed by bacteria to the point of making it inedible for the rest of us. But then I thought: wait, this food doesn't need to spoil, regardless of the working status of the fridge. I've been canning stuff the last two months, and there's nothing in that freezer that can't be canned: chickens, fish, beef, vegetables, a gallon of stew in plastic yogurt containers. I can do all that this evening, if I have enough jars left over from canning applesauce, pears, tomatoes, fruit butters, tuna, and four quarts of potato-leek soup.

Revision:
During the night our refrigerator stopped working. Not without warning exactly. The last time this happened, several months ago, I gave it a sharp jolt with the side of my fist and it started running again, like nothing had happened. I started to believe it might be OK. Now it's six A.M., the refrigerator is off, the freezer full of food is defrosting, and it is a problem that will have to wait until this afternoon.

At first I felt a moment of panic, with the thought of fifty dollars of food being consumed by bacteria. But then I thought: I've been canning stuff the last two months, and there's nothing in that freezer that can't be canned: chickens, fish, beef, vegetables, a gallon of stew in plastic yogurt containers. I can do all that this evening, if I have enough jars left over from canning applesauce, pears, tomatoes, fruit butters, tuna, and four quarts of potato-leek soup.

The smooth narrative rhythm works well in the original. It's just slowed down in places by unnecessary exposition of facts, facts we really don't need to know. And the notion of forcing the cooperation of an appliance is a little hackneyed. The revision simply streamlines the original, cutting out what doesn't work, making what does work stand out more.

And this from Eric's sketchbook.

Style is the careful use of distinctive words or writing forms that contributes to the message of the piece of writing. Isn't it? It seems that style is a very difficult concept to pin down. It defies definition, like pornography. I sure know it when I see it. Or is rhetoric empty and meaningless except when you are in school, and then it is all? Most of the time it is defined as the opposite by its opposite. This piece has no stylistic resonance. It just lies there on the page. What makes words able to do anything but stain the page? Lie inky on the page? Break up the monotony of a white page? Or do they just make it two tone? It is easier to pinpoint style in a speaker. The words are taken, lifted off the page by a breath, by a voice. The voice can then let the words drift away, send them like an arrow through the heart, drop them over the podium to squish the listeners, crash down on the audience accompanied with fire and brimstone. Speaking style must be very similar to writing style. Can written words drift, send, drop, and crash? I'm not sure, but I'd know it if I saw it.

Style assumes some kind of conscious control of language and more specifically, written language. The idea seems to be that the author has some ability to craft his writing to mean more than it says, to mean more than the definition of the words. The concept that the writer just furnishes the words and they interact with the reader to create their own meaning doesn't seem to account for style. Hemingway had a very distinct style. He did not write so much as he crafted, created. He was an artist. But, many times his work looked and felt crafted or created. That still is a distinctive style. Fitzgerald also had a style. There are contests that award prizes on the ability to copy Hemingway's and Fitzgerald's styles. The judges must know what style is when they see it. . . .

Revision:

What makes words able to do anything but stain the page, lie inky on the page? What breaks up the monotony of a white page? Or do words just make it two tone?

It's easier to pinpoint in a speaker. There words are taken, lifted off the page by a breath, a voice. The voice can then let the words drift away, send them like an arrow through the heart, drop them over the podium to squish the listeners, crash down on the audience accompanied with fire and brimstone. Can written words drift, send, drop, and crash?

The idea seems to be that the author has some ability to craft his writing to mean more than it says, to mean more than the definition of the words.

I include this example to show the process of radical cutting and revising. It's a freewrite, the writer thinking through the problem as he writes, and much of the language of it is simply rambling, beside the point, soft and blurry. The key is to keep what's good, what's strong here, eliminating all the rest and then blending the good pieces together. Some paragraphing is necessary, too. What I keep is the concrete, the earthy, the vivid.

THE DANGERS OF UTILITY

But you can go too far in revising for economy and clarity alone, making the writing tight and mincing, tightening yourself up as you compose and revise the next piece. The concerns of economy, if taken too far, can lead to a distrust of all language and style, the desire to eliminate all connotation as inefficient and achieve some kind of neutral, unambiguous phrase for each idea. That's not possible, the world being too complex, language being too unstable. It's also not desirable. What the striving for absolute clarity fails to understand is the great richness of language simply as sound. The power of words comes not only or even primarily from their capacity to communicate an idea but far more from intangible sources of connotation and playfulness and emotional suggestiveness. Writing that works is writing that not only gets an idea across but also a feeling or sound or rhythm.

Anne should cut out "definitely" not because it's inefficient but because the sentence *sounds* better without it. It's better not because its content is any clearer that way but because rhythmically it's cleaner and less predictable.

What this means practically is that you need to check the question "What should I cut?" with "What sounds good?" You need to revise by keeping track both of meanings and of "glows."

The choice is never between clarity and style. When you describe a forest as a "multiple-output commercial asset," you're not just conveying a neutral meaning. You're conveying a tone, a glow, a feeling, too—a tone *of* objectivity in this case. The phrase is multiple-outputlike itself, suggesting a computer or economic system, images of spreadsheets pouring out of dot-matrix printers. Calling a forest a "forest" suggests something more organic, green, living. Deciding which of these terms to use is not a decision based solely on clarity—although meaning is of course involved—but on rhetoric and style, too, the sense of the forest you want to convey.

There are times when you legitimately want and need to sound more "multiple-outputlike" than "forestlike," in scientific papers, for example, or at conferences and business meetings. But that's just the point. Your choice of this language is as much determined by the need to *sound* a certain way—a member of this club, a person in this role—as it is by meaning.

ASSONANCE, CONSONANCE, AND ALLITERATION

*T*his power of sound and feel, for example, is connected to the effect of vowels and consonants:

Assonance: the sound of vowels
the yellow fields and the cottonwoods and the rivers rising and falling and the mountain roads closing when the heavy snow comes in

(and: yellow and roads and closing and snow)

standing, swiveling flabbergasted, feeling exultation and the rush of friendship

Consonance: the sound of consonants
a *sen*se of her cou*sin*s and of river*s* and of her great grandmother*'s* tea-
cup*s*

(and: he*r*, river*s*, he*r*, and grandmothe*r*)

swep*t* off my fee*t*, I floa*t*ed from one side to the other, swiveling my
brain, *s*taring a*s*tounded a*t* the beavers, then the o*tt*ers

(and: *off, f*eet, *f*loated; *f*loated, swive*l*ing; *s*wept, *s*ide, *s*wiveling, *s*taring,
a*s*tounded, beaver*s*, otter*s*; othe*r*, beaver*s*, otte*rs*)

Alliteration: beginning each word with the same consonant
*d*ifficult, oblique, *d*eliberately inarticulate

*s*tanding, *s*wiveling *f*labbergasted, *f*eeling exultation and a rush of *f*riend-
ship

Prose writers use devices of sound more subtly than poets, weaving
together patterns of assonance and consonance to intensify language at
important moments. Sometimes there are even rhymes or near
rhymes—sensation, elation, perfection; yellow, roads, closing, snow—
but they're never so noticeable, in effective pieces, that the writing
sounds singsong or forced. The patterns are below the surface, worked
into the rhythm of the sentences. The effect is to throw some words and
phrases into slight relief, make them sound just a little deeper and
richer, seem more vivid.

The effect, too, is to create a mood or feel. There is a melodiousness and flow in Didion's "cottonwoods" line, its sounds all soothing and sonorous: the "-ings" repeated, the mellow *o* sounds, the
smoothing *s* sounds, the *f*s and the *v*s. A similar melodiousness
explains the feel of Thomas's "swiveling flabbergasted" phrase. In
contrast:

> Our look was as if two lovers, or deadly enemies, met unexpectedly
> on an overgrown path when each had been thinking of something else:
> a clearing blow to the gut. It was also a bright blow to the brain, or a
> sudden beating of brains, with all the charge and intimate grate of
> rubbed balloons.

In "*b*right *b*low to the *b*rain" Dillard relies on alliteration to create the
sensation of bright blowing she felt when she first saw a weasel face to

face. "Gut" and "grate" have a distant alliterative effect and a hard, sharp brevity. The language in all these phrases sounds in some general way like what it's describing, harsh sounds for harsh experiences, musical sounds for moments of pleasure and nostalgia.

Power comes not only through deliberate alliteration or near rhyming, the relation of sounds in a series of words, but also through the sound or feel of individual words in and of themselves. "Slats" seems to me a pleasing word, more pleasing here than a phrase like "vertical cylinders of wood" or even, less obviously, "bars." At least it has a different quality on the page than "bars" or "cylinders," which may be fine and effective words in other situations. Its one syllable emphatic, the *sl* sliding into a strong *t*. Thomas's "flattened" and "flabbergasted" has something of that same effect.

Orwell favored Anglo-Saxon words, words from the earliest roots of English as language, to Latinate additions made later. Both "slats" and "flattened" are Old English in origin. But looking at assonance and consonance can also lead to an appreciation of phrases like "viewshed" (after all)—the vague-sounding "view" blending with the more concrete "shed," echoing the geographic overtones of "watershed," also a pleasing word. From the perspective of sound alone, much of the wonderland of disciplinary jargon becomes intriguing. There are "edge effects" in forestry, too, or "snag configurations," or "whorl patterns." Many Latinate words sound interesting in their own right and can work well in contexts—"exultation" in Thomas, for example.

Thomas often mixes earthy Old English words and scientific abstractions: "shouts across the corpus callosum"; "display receptors" leading to the feeling of being "flabbergasted." The implicit suggestion is that these two realms and ways of thinking are connected—the theme of the essay.

The number of syllables within and across words has some bearing on sound, too. The question is what combination of hard and soft, accented and unaccented syllables sounds best. In its three accented words, "bright blow to the brain" has an effective staccato sound, it seems to me, whereas the Didion line would be ruined by scrambling the series: "yellow fields and the cottonwoods and the mountain roads closing when the heavy snow comes in and the rivers rising and falling." The "mountain roads" part of the phrase is the longest, the only one with subordinate modification, and so it has to complete the phrase.

"Comes in" as a final sound to the sentence is more fulfilling, more satisfying here, than "falling."

THE POWER OF METAPHOR

*A*nother source of connotative power is metaphor, a concrete *vehicle* conveying a *tenor* or idea:

, My love (the tenor) is a red red rose (the vehicle).

A simile is an explicit metaphor:

My love is like a red, red rose.

The power of metaphor is that it means more than it says. When I say my love is a red, red rose, I do not mean that I'm in love with a rose. I mean that my love is beautiful, perfect, fragile, temporary, full of thorns, growing. I mean something that, literally, I didn't say. The concrete image is capable of packing in layers and layers of meaning, of intensifying the glow of words.

A metaphor also has the power of concreteness. The sensory qualities of the vehicle appear on the page, entering into our minds as we read. We feel roses, remember their scents. We are back in the world of living, felt things again. A metaphor mingles that felt world with the world of ideas and meanings. The implicit assertion is that some meaning—love—has in some ways the qualities of the vehicle—a rose.

Metaphors are perhaps the most effective ways writers have to make an idea "present" in the minds of readers. They not only communicate something unknown or elusive by something known and familiar—not only clarify ideas in graspable ways—but also bring ideas alive, make them vital and real.

Dillard experiences the sight of the weasel as a physical blow, sudden and leveling, unpleasant ("grate") but also purifying ("clearing"). Didion writes of the "guerrilla war" in her family, the "ambushes" of family life, suggesting surreptitious, underground combat. Thomas writes of ideas and feelings "shouting" across the corpus callosum, as if the hemispheres of his brain are people and the barrier between them a wall. The image suggests an exuberant effort to overcome division. Ants exchange "memoranda" for Thomas, much like people in an office. The cooperation of ants is an extended metaphor for human relationships, just as the visit to the overturned gravestones in "On Going Home" is an extended metaphor for family tradition, shared history, becoming lost and forgotten. (There is a snake in this garden, too—danger, evil.)

Metaphors don't prove ideas. They are efficient in the sense that they can compress a great deal of meaning into a short space, but inefficient in the sense that they don't convey new information. The weasel is stunning, family relations strained, the beavers and otters marvelous. We *know* that without the metaphors and images. We just don't *feel* it.

All language depends on metaphor. We can't seem to think except by comparison of ideas and of ideas with things and events in the natural world—this is like that, this happened before and now it's happening again, these things are related. Metaphors become so embedded in our language that we use them all the time without know it. Just look at the last few paragraphs: "embedded," "power," "compress." Often metaphors lose their power through repeated use, becoming clichéd or dead, and so have to be replaced. Too many projects have been "launched," too many "waves" made, too many "courses charted."

"Bright blows to the brain" can change that, and "guerrilla" warfare. We need more shouts across the corpus callosum.

SPONTANEITY AND CRAFT

*M*etaphors and patterns of sound are often the product of conscious crafting. You have to turn a word over and over in your mind or rewrite a phrase again and again until you manage to invoke the experience. Crafting like this is a pleasure when it comes not out of a desire to inflate and impress but from a felt need to say something; when it's grounded in the natural patterns of speech and thinking; when the result isn't pat and predictable and too familiar.

Often, too, this kind of richness of phrasing happens spontaneously as you write. From a recent set of student freewritings:

My mind drifts from time to time to my excursion to the unknown arms awaiting me in Independence. In Adair Village is where I usually take off.

I can only see the hedge and the sky, nothing else.

Pick and snap. Meme would can. Boil the apples, mash the apples, add sugar, cinnamon, pour. I can taste it, sweet, cool, a little lumpy.

Shrooms. Let's not forget shrooms. Wedges of wonderful food.

Raking leaves in the twilight, dusk, after dark. All three tree's worth.

Wild array of plants.

Oh God, they're taking off my top!

Déjà vu delicacy.

What *was* the name of my first grade true love? Jimmy Spores, of course!

Hambo nirvana.

The dance is so spinnerly, so rounding, so dizzying.

Following dreams costs.

Ease is not necessarily best.

These are just phrases that attracted my attention by their sound and feel. Scanning the freewriting, I allowed myself to look only at surfaces, simply to underline whatever seemed interesting for whatever reason.

An extended exercise in verbal play (a revised student free-writing):

```
     Feed.   Misfeed.   Feedback.   Missed   loop . . .
loopy?--aren't we all. Hmmm . . . does this mean
sense, logic, content, meaningful dialogue, dis-
course, recourse, intercourse, undercourse, cor-
sets are out the window? I'm trying to grasp the
implications of this sound-only sensitivity (un-
sound wallowing?) Wallow. What a great word--it
rings of emptiness, like ''hollow,'' and at the
same time, it seems to invite one to settle in,
relax, roll around, imitate a buffalo--go ahead;
don't be shy. How does it feel? Oozey! Feel the
```

pleasantly oozing feelings, between your toes, around your legs, warm and gooey. When you sit in a wallow, it's like sitting in a giant Pampers diaper that wasn't changed in time. It sort of contradicts the whole idea of being pampered, though. Pampers, prams, prognostication, prosthesis, proboscus, pronounce (a hard word to pronounciate, as many people will demonstrate). This is the wallow of language. Wallow . . . wallow . . . wallow . . . I'm hitting the wallow. Wall—o? That's what runners do, is hit the wall—o They run themselves to the point of exhaustion, hit the wall—o, and bang! the wall—o is broken. That's like the word wallow, too. Wallows grab you; they suck at your feet, make your footing so slimy that it's hard not to wallow in the wallow, whether you plan to or not. On the other side of a good wallow, though, you feel refreshed, wholesome, rejuvenated, ready to run the next 10 kilometers without feeling much pain. It's no wonder we like to wallow. It's animal nature, human nature, the nature of life to want to wallow. I think I'll try to devolve. I'll work at enjoying a mud bath——a wallow that is physically satisfying, rather than mentally muddling. I'll offset the frustration of wallowing in academica by wallowing in nature. I'm off to satisfy my animal instincts. Annie Dillard says to live like a weasel but I'd rather wallow like a hippo.

The jargon and the inflating of officious and academic writers comes not from love of language but from fear of it. Anne doesn't use "purchase" out of a delight in its sound but out of her uneasiness writing to a new teacher. The rollicking writer doesn't use "rollicking" because he appreciates the sound of words but because he regards words as disposable. These are throwaway lines, fast-food phrases. Easy come, easy go.

But "hambo nirvana" and "deja vu delicacy" are just fun, a delighting in sound. The wallowing writer wallows not to deceive but to play and explore, not thinking about the language but about the experiences underneath, or thinking about the language for the sake of the language, not for the sake of impressing the reader. These are interesting and surprising phrasings, too, not hackneyed and clichéd. The usual pairings and balances are upset here, the conventional rhythms effectively thrown off.

The theory of "tropes" is that style is distortion, a warping of the normal flow of language. Literally, a trope is the turning or twisting of language into more intense or unusual patterns. The words that strike us in these pieces of freewriting have that quality of the unusual, of the interestingly distorted. We attend to them because there is a special energy or rhythm in them, some surplus of value.

Maybe the power is accidental. Maybe it's syntax taking over and the words taking charge, coming out and coming out, the sound patterns the product of chance or a kind of unthinking fulfillment of syntactical logic. Still the words move and grow. Still there's the power and the surprise, whatever its origins.

Here is one of Anne's freewrites from later in the term, not playful and hamming it up but earnest, struggling to get a meaning right:

> Start a new section—turning, spading, breaking clods, pulling weed root wads, dirt under my fingernails, bark dust slivers, surprises under the soil, smells. I want full, prolific gardens. I want interest. I want contentment. I want sunshine. I want time. I want creativity. I want happiness. I want. I want. I want. My home, my garden, my life, my husband. Tied to the earth. Fragrant, rotting, evolving, renewing, regenerating, repeating, repeating, repeating. The hoe, the claw thing, my gloves, my shears/clippers. Tools to work the earth.

You start at one pole of the spectrum and end up on the other side. You begin by rejecting all phoniness and artful stylishness, letting the words come as they need to come, and when you let that energy take over, have its way, you eventually find yourself back in the realm of the stylized and the artful, the realm of that which calls attention to itself: "weed root wads," "repeating, repeating, repeating." But that stylishness is organic now, part of the natural rhythm of your thinking and feeling, and interesting because different, not predictable, imitating in some way the fullness and eddying and recalcitrance of the experience always beyond the words.

In the epigram to this chapter Wallace Stevens suggests that the harder you try to express your deepest meanings, the more the sounds of words matter to you—the more you "search" these sounds, try to feel for the right one. True stylishness comes not from the effort to hide meaning but from the effort to reveal it. The distortions of style reflect the struggling of the mind as it moves deep down into the richness and messiness of experience itself.

THE USEFULNESS OF EXTREMES

*W*allowing is good for experiencing the possibilities of language. You come out the other side feeling refreshed, rejuvenated, ready for the next 10 kilometers. You come out knowing something more about the connotative power that all words possess to one degree or another.

More on this in the last chapter. For now, let me go back to the writing we started with at the beginning of the chapter and recombine the practical perspectives of economy and sound:

I purchased a spiral notebook so I can write wherever I am

should be revised as either

I bought a spiral notebook so I can write wherever I am

or

I purchased a spiral notebook—plain and beige, but portable, 7¾ by 5, the spiraling binder somehow satisfying—hoping thereby to gain some purchase on my style, some hold on the thoughts that appear spontaneously in my mind, capturing and fixing them there for revision later.

Both revisions are examples of the free/style: the first in the sense of writing more like you talk, more like you are; the second in the sense of a kind of verbal gymnastics and showing off, a pushing for greater stylistic power, no holds barred. Writing the free/style, in short, means pushing your language to either side of that awkward opening sentence, revising it downward or upward, and feeling comfortable in both directions, in control.

It means attending to the sound of words, which is always the issue for writers and readers, even in a simple memo:

> On the 15th of this month Standard Insurance will be implementing a new program: The Feedback Box.
>
> It's a chance for you to tell us about problems or offer kudos for management.
>
> Just write out your comment on a single sheet of paper—typed or handwritten is fine—and slip it in. The management will read all the cards and then award $100 to $500 cash bonuses for the best suggestion, morale booster, money saver, helpful hint.
>
> This is a great opportunity to learn some new things and work on some old—and to keep with our tradition of Associates' concerns first.

This was freewritten in about five minutes, revised in another five using COAP. Nothing obviously fancy here. No elaborate introduction or attempt to advertise. That wouldn't be appropriate in a company where everyone expects to get memos from management and a great deal of information is exchanged each day. Short and sweet is best. Just the facts.

But some of the words glow, too: "kudos," "sheet," "slip," "fine," "booster," "saver." There's some life here, some pieces of real experience. The image of the writer we get is of someone down to earth and to the point. We get the sense that maybe management really does want some suggestions, isn't just saying it.

This is the effect that free/style strives for, an effect not of plainness but of energy and authenticity.

SKETCHBOOK

✐ My sketchbook suggestion for the next four chapters is to observe and record the language you encounter every day in your reading and work and conversations, studying its sounds and structures. If you're finding freewriting comfortable and productive, by all means keep doing it. "Wallowing" would be a good exercise for this chapter, for example, just going all out in a freewrite and playing with sounds. But for the next four chapters I'd like you to turn your attention mostly outward, becoming conscious of language as language.

For this chapter: observe and record the diction all around you, the words and phrases that you read and hear in your daily life. Make a glossary of those that seem problematic or beautiful or otherwise important:

> · jargon on the job or in your discipline, words that at one time sounded odd to you when you first heard them but that seem natural now; words that still seem unnatural or uncomfortable
> · jargon and abstraction and difficult diction you encounter outside your own area of expertise, words you are in the process of learning
> · words and phrases that seem pompous, inflated, dishonest, distancing, unnecessarily abstract, stilted
> · metaphors, subtle or obvious
> · any words or phrases that strike you as especially beautiful or sonorous or knotty or textured, words that resonate

Define these words if you need to. Revise and simplify the ugly and abstract. Reflect on their purposes and audiences, the motives behind them. Keep track of all this in your own writing, too, whatever kind you're doing, skimming off the interesting or difficult surfaces.

R E V I S I O N

✐ Revise the first or second practice piece again, in light of the discussion in this chapter. Cut, deflate, shape, craft.

I'll be suggesting you do this at the end of each of the next four chapters: revise either of these pieces, in light of that discussion, looking just at those issues.

Further revising one or two pieces from several angles is artificial, of course (although often an essay does have to be revised many, many times). It's just a way of slowing down the process one time through, separating out all the related elements one by one so that you can see them clearly. You may find in this chapter, for example, that in your first rough draft of one of the practice pieces, you've already, intuitively, through COAP, cut out much of the pompous and inflated diction. Or you'll have gone part of the way the first time and then will have to shape and build the rest.

I say revise *either* the first or second practice piece over the next four chapters because you may exhaust the possibilities of just one. But it may be that one of your practice pieces will hold up to four different kinds of attention and that it will be simpler to stick with it throughout. You could even freewrite and COAP all new pieces for each chapter—or apply my advice to a single long piece you'd already written before you started reading this book and now just have to revise and polish.

•••••••••••••••••••••••••••••••••••

4

THE SHAPE OF CONTENT

Some people, I guess, thrive by deferring to unknown and presumably higher authority, to the benevolence of vast, indistinct institutions. And of course, it's never a simple matter when your life requires submitting to the judgment of others. We all accommodate that. But most of the writers I have respected and still respect seem to me not so adept at discerning and respecting underlying design, but actually spend all their efforts trying to invent designs anew. What [is] out there . . . is not a structure for writers to surrender to, but fidgety, dodgy chaos. And our privileged task is to force it, calm it to our wills.

—Richard Ford, introduction to *The Pushcart Prize: Best of the Small Presses, 1988–1989*

*I*n the all-at-onceness of revising, the balancing act of trying to make the words and the ideas work, you're always going back and forth from the small to the large, the little details to the grand design. You're thinking about questions of overall structure and coherence at the same moment you're worrying over individual words and phrases, cutting out an adverb here, strengthening a verb there.

FORM AND CONTENT

*T*here isn't any single logic for mastering formal problems, just the hard work of writing and revising as you try to say what you need and want to say. "Form is the shape of content," to quote William Irmscher quoting the artist Ben Shahn. If you have two points to make, for example, there's hardly any way to avoid a sequential structure of twos: my first point is, my second point is (explicitly or implicitly). If you have two ideas to compare and contrast, you naturally have to make decisions about whether to alternate comparisons under certain headings or say everything about *A* first, then everything about *B*. Transitions get blurry and points scrambled when you're unclear about the subject matter, either because you haven't done your homework or because you're still struggling to understand a complex subject.

The best way to find the appropriate structure for any piece of writing is through the act of writing, discovering form as you write and then revising to incorporate what you've discovered. Outline first. Sketch and doodle. But don't get discouraged when it turns out you have to revise the draft anyway. You just can't figure out transitions until you're down there in the middle of the words and ideas actually trying to move from one paragraph to the next.

INDENTATION AS INTERPRETATION

*O*ne approach to understanding this relationship between form and content is by way of the paragraph, a graphic indication of the movement of an essay from point to point.

Paragraphing moves from the outside in rather than from the inside out. Indentation is interpretation, to paraphrase Paul Rodgers, a way of signaling changes in the flow of the writing as it moves from the beginning to the end.

Form and structure work globally rather than locally. When you write, you don't build from the ground level up, making form out of individual sentences and paragraphs like little building blocks, mechanically assembling pieces. You begin with a gestalt, a sense of the conceptual and structural rhythm of a whole piece of writing, and you write the individual sentences in light of that gestalt, which then changes as a result of the momentum and energy and surprises of the sentences as they actually come out on the screen.

Paragraphing comes intuitively in this process, as you write. The indentations mark shifts in direction, emphasis, and rhythm.

A freewrite:

```
A voice that speaks carries you along with it
without pushing, without holding you back. It
doesn't drown you in the rapids, doesn't allow you
to just barely hold on while you get dunked over
and over again. It may give you a freezing splash
in the face but that doesn't happen for any par-
ticular reason. I see now the reason that essay,
assay--to try, to attempt--if it were cut and
dried, if it did not involve effort, process,
structure, then there would be no need to ''try.''
Trying is the means by which one scouts out the
place, rustles around the underbrush for snakes.
It's really pretty exciting to explore and if
things were perfect--I think the voice is plucked
not by perfection but by knowing perfection or
near perfection was achieved through the effort
you gave birth to, by the effort you created, the
effort you had a reason to ''assiyez.'' I some-
times think my voice is very deep within me and
when people see you ''trying'' to bring it forth,
it (you) lose that mystique, that guise of ef-
fortlessness. There are so many different worlds,
all intersecting; voice is when you get different
and sometimes even discordant worlds to intersect
```

without creating tidal waves but creating waves, slow resonant waves move, the water stands still, the waves move endlessly, breaking apart the little water molecules and reforming them, again broken, again re-formed. The waves do it all. Easy waves, no tidal waves. Some people's speaking voices are like that, they lull you, the voice sweeps you into its own pattern and helps you believe you agree with everything it says. Voice takes you to the heart. The heart beats, it doesn't move, it moves the blood, but it just keeps going around and around, beating slowly, beating fast, palpitating, beating, never stopping, constant change and tension, never varying, no audience. Voice is the harmony between what you say and how you say it. There is the surface harmony as when you have conflict and agree to let it drop but still seethe underneath. There is harmony from no tension, just a placid, pleasant, complacent smile--that enigmatic Mona Lisa that means nothing to no one. Voice is not diffident, voice is not flashy, seductive, one-time words. Voice is not hoping someone won't call you arrogant or uppity for your opinions. Voice is not a hammer, it is not convincing but persuading. Voice is not a small tiny peeping in a big room. It is a face that fills up the space. It is content that fills up form. It is when the conscious can merge with the subconscious. It is when you are caught off guard and you say the right thing without ever having to struggle. Because it's in there; you didn't have time to put your sensing cap on--you let the intuition out through a tiny little pinhole leak before you could get your finger back up over it.

Deciding where to indent in this piece of writing—unparagraphed in its original form—is a way of simulating the outside-in experience of paragraphing:

A voice that speaks carries you along with it without pushing, without holding you back. It doesn't drown you in the rapids, doesn't allow you to just barely hold on while you get dunked over and over again. It may give you a freezing splash in the face but that doesn't happen for any particular reason.

I see now the reason that essay, assay--to try, to attempt--if it were cut and dried, if it did not involve effort, process, structure, then there would be no need to ''try.'' Trying is the means by which one scouts out the place, rustles around the underbrush for snakes. It's really pretty exciting to explore and if things were perfect--I think the voice is plucked not by perfection but by knowing perfection or near perfection was achieved through the effort you gave birth to, by the effort you created, the effort you had a reason to ''assiyez.'' I sometimes think my voice is very deep within me and when people see you ''trying'' to bring it forth, it (you) lose that mystique, that guise of effortlessness.

There are so many different worlds, all intersecting; voice is when you get different and sometimes even discordant worlds to intersect without creating tidal waves but creating waves, slow resonant waves move, the water stands still, the waves move endlessly, breaking apart the little water molecules and reforming them, again broken, again re-formed. The waves do it all. Easy waves, no tidal waves. Some people's speaking voices are like that, they lull you, the voice sweeps you into its own pattern and helps you believe you agree with everything it says.

Voice takes you to the heart. The heart beats, it doesn't move, it moves the blood, but it just keeps going around and around, beating slowly, beating fast, palpitating, beating, never stopping, constant change and tension, never varying, no audience.

Voice is the harmony between what you say and how you say it. There is the surface harmony as

when you have conflict and agree to let it drop but
still seethe underneath. There is harmony from
no tension, just a placid, pleasant, complacent
smile--that enigmatic Mona Lisa that means nothing
to no one.

    Voice is not diffident, voice is not flashy,
seductive, one-time words. Voice is not hoping
someone won't call you arrogant or uppity for your
opinions. Voice is not a hammer, it is not convincing but persuading. Voice is not a small tiny
peeping in a big room. It is a face that fills up
the space. It is content that fills up form. It is
when the conscious can merge with the subconscious. It is when you are caught off guard and you
say the right thing without ever having to struggle. Because it's in there; you didn't have time to
put your sensing cap on--you let the intuition out
through a tiny little pinhole leak before you
could get your finger back up over it.

It makes sense to indent at "I see." The movement at this point is from
"a voice" to "I," from metaphorical assertion to analysis of those metaphors. And the rhythm of the sentences changes here, too, from steady,
direct statement to more subordination and interior modification. It
makes sense to paragraph again at "There are so many different worlds,
all intersecting," not only because the writing moves away from "I"
again but because this statement introduces the extended metaphor of
"waves." It makes sense to indent at "Voice takes you to the heart"
because it introduces another metaphor.

    The underlying structure of this piece is a series of definitions of
the idea of voice—a repetitive structure depending largely on assertion
and metaphor. Paragraphing can reveal the more obvious shifts to new
attempts at definition.

RHETORICAL PARAGRAPHING

*P*aragraphing is rhetorical, a matter
of what you want to emphasize. That is, there's more than one acceptable way of paragraphing any piece of writing:

A voice that speaks carries you along with it without pushing, without holding you back. It doesn't drown you in the rapids, doesn't allow you to just barely hold on while you get dunked over and over again. It may give you a freezing splash in the face but that doesn't happen for any particular reason.

I see now the reason that essay, assay—to try, to attempt—if it were cut and dried, if it did not involve effort, process, structure, then there would be no need to ''try.'' Trying is the means by which one scouts out the place, rustles around the underbrush for snakes. It's really pretty exciting to explore and if things were perfect—I think the voice is plucked not by perfection but by knowing perfection or near perfection was achieved through the effort you gave birth to, by the effort you created, the effort you had a reason to ''assiyez.''

I sometimes think my voice is very deep within me and when people see you ''trying'' to bring it forth, it (you) lose that mystique, that guise of effortlessness.

There are so many different worlds, all intersecting; voice is when you get different and sometimes even discordant worlds to intersect without creating tidal waves but creating waves, slow resonant waves move, the water stands still, the waves move endlessly, breaking apart the little water molecules and reforming them, again broken, again re-formed. The waves do it all. Easy waves, no tidal waves. Some people's speaking voices are like that, they lull you, the voice sweeps you into its own pattern and helps you believe you agree with everything it says.

Voice takes you to the heart. The heart beats, it doesn't move, it moves the blood, but it just keeps going around and around, beating slowly, beating fast, palpitating, beating, never stopping, constant change and tension, never varying, no audience.

> Voice is the harmony between what you say and how you say it. There is the surface harmony as when you have conflict and agree to let it drop but still see the underneath. There is harmony from no tension, just a placid, pleasant, complacent smile—that enigmatic Mona Lisa that means nothing to no one.
>
> Voice is not diffident, voice is not flashy, seductive, one-time words. Voice is not hoping someone won't call you arrogant or uppity for your opinions. Voice is not a hammer, it is not convincing but persuading.
>
> Voice is not a small tiny peeping in a big room. It is a face that fills up the space. It is content that fills up form. It is when the conscious can merge with the subconscious.
>
> It is when you are caught off guard and you say the right thing without ever having to struggle. Because it's in there; you didn't have time to put your sensing cap on—you let the intuition out through a tiny little pinhole leak before you could get your finger back up over it.

Making "I sometimes think my voice is very deep within me" a one-sentence paragraph highlights that statement, giving it a more important status in the composition. It has more the weight of a thesis statement in this version, while in the first version it was subordinated in a sequence of analytical statements.

Paragraphing reflects meaning. There's an argument for leaving the freewriting without any indentations at all. That would help indicate graphically the sense of spilling out, the rush of energy, the writing projects. There's also an argument for creating many short paragraphs, as I do in the last part of this second version, breaking at each major shift in metaphor. That helps reinforce the sense of repeated definition, the piling up of alternatives.

Visual spacing and variety are a part of paragraphing. Just as you don't want to have too many short sentences or too many long sentences one after the other, you don't want too many long or short paragraphs in succession, unless you're deliberately trying to create a choppy, rapid-fire organizational scheme. My first paragraphed version moves steadily from medium-sized paragraph to medium-sized paragraph; the second begins steadily and then breaks up into shorter pieces.

This means, too, that one-sentence paragraphs are legal. You don't want to have too many, or they lose their effectiveness, which depends on contrast, the presence of longer paragraphs on either side. But once you start viewing paragraphs in their rhetorical relationships to each other, you realize that one-sentence paragraphs can be very useful as ways of making transitions or emphasizing key points.

PARAGRAPH BLOCS

*P*aragraphs function together as "blocs" within a piece of writing, clustering around themes and meanings in larger multiparagraph units. A thesis statement in the first paragraph may govern five or six or any number of subsequent paragraphs.

This is of course true in longer pieces of writing, long articles or essays and the chapters of books, where groups of paragraphs work together like subessays within the larger whole. (In this book these chunks or blocs are obvious from the subheadings I use to separate them.) After the opening paragraph, "The Tucson Zoo" falls into two obvious blocs, the first centered on the beavers and otters, the experience and the reflection on that experience; the second centered on the analogy of ants, the question of altruism versus grabbiness. The five paragraphs of the first bloc are controlled, in effect, by "I had a brief, personal experience of this misgiving." The four paragraphs of the second are controlled by an "assembled" topic sentence consisting of "Everyone says, stay away from ants"—and the "point of view" this represents—and "but this is a hard argument to make."

Seeing a paragraph as simply a miniessay, a self-contained unit, can't account for the complexity of these balanced, interwoven structures.

TOPIC SENTENCES

*N*ot all paragraphs have topic sentences. In an empirical study of nonfiction prose, "The Frequency and

Placement of Topic Sentences in Expository Prose," Richard Braddock found that the paragraphs of published writers—academic, technical, and professional—actually have initial topic sentences only 13 percent of the time. (Irmscher puts that number at more like 40 or 50 percent.) In the rest of their paragraphs the topic sentences come in the middle or at the end, are implied rather than stated, are assembled—part stated in the middle and then completed at the end—or are simply absent altogether, the paragraph governed by the statement of theme in an earlier paragraph in the bloc.

The last four paragraphs of "On Going Home," for example, are governed by the restatement of the thesis in the first paragraph of that bloc, "That I am trapped in this particular irrelevancy is never more apparent to me than when I go home." The other three paragraphs in the bloc have no topic sentences at all, are just parallel illustrations.

This paragraph from "The Tucson Zoo" has a thesis in the middle, a turning point or pivot:

> Sometimes people argue this point of view seriously and with deep thought. Be individuals, solitary and selfish, is the message. Altruism, a jargon word for what used to be called love, is worse than weakness, it is a sin, a violation of nature. Be separate. Do not be a social animal. *But this is a hard argument to make convincingly when you have to depend on language to make it.* You have to print up leaflets or publish books and get them bought and sent around, you have to turn up on television and catch the attention of millions of other human beings all at once, and then you have to say to all of them, all at once, all collected and paying attention: be solitary; do not depend on each other. You can't do this and keep a straight face.

Perhaps the way to understand this paragraph is to think of the thesis statement as coming in two parts, the first at the beginning and the second in the middle: "sometimes people argue . . . but this is a hard argument to make." In any event, the flow and movement of this paragraph is more complex—more natural—than the conventional advice about paragraphing can indicate.

A lot of the lore of paragraphing has been invented by nonwriters for the purposes of teachability. It's easier to explain that a paragraph is always a miniessay with this exact number of parts coming in this exact order. It just doesn't happen to be true.

INSIDE PARAGRAPHS
••••••••••••••••••••••••••••••••

This isn't to say that there isn't some value in the notion that paragraphs are like miniessays, the parts illustrating or developing a particular idea. Generally (just not necessarily or mechanically), they are. The principle of paragraphing is the principle of development. What takes up the space in a paragraph are explanations and illustrations and unpacking of a generalization.

It's useful to look at the paragraph from the inside out, too, in other words, as long as you keep the outside-in perspective in mind as a check. The local and global levels of paragraphing mirror and influence each other, exist in a constructive tension.

One way of understanding the paragraph internally is to think of it as having a cumulative structure analogous to the structure of the cumulative sentence (I'll be talking about cumulative sentences in the next chapter):

I am home for my daughter's first birthday.

> By home I do not mean the house in Los Angeles where my husband and I and the baby live, but the place where my family is, in the Central Valley of California.

> > It is a vital, although troublesome distinction.

> > My husband likes my family but is uneasy in their house, because once there I fall into their ways, which are difficult, oblique, deliberately inarticulate, not my husband's ways.

> > > We live in dusty houses ("D-U-S-T," he once wrote with his finger on surfaces all over the house, but no one noticed it) filled with mementos quite without value to him (what could the Canton dessert plates mean to him? how could he have known about the assay scales, why should he care if he did know?), and we appear to talk exclusively about people we know who have been booked on drunk-driving charges, and about property, particularly about property, land, price per acre and C-2 zoning and assessments and freeway access.

My brother does not understand my husband's inability to perceive the advantage in the rather common real-estate transaction known as "sale-leaseback," and my husband in turn does not understand why so many of the people he hears about in my father's house have recently been committed to mental hospitals or booked on drunk-driving charges.

Nor does he understand that when we talk about sale-leasebacks and right-of-way condemnations we are talking in code about the things we like best, the yellow fields and the cottonwoods and the rivers rising and falling and the mountain roads closing when the heavy snow comes in.

> We miss each other's points, have another drink and regard the fire.

My brother refers to my husband, in his presence, as "Joan's husband."

Marriage is the classic betrayal.

I've indented further to the right the more particular or developed the sentence has seemed to be. All of them are subordinate to the opening statement of the topic "home," ebbing and flowing beneath that generalization, providing texture and detail, explanation, just as the modifiers of the cumulative sentence refine and extend the main clause. There's movement in both directions within the paragraph, toward the particular and away. "We miss each other's points," for example, is a sentence giving more particular detail for the "sale-leasebacks" sentence before, and then the paragraph moves back out in "My brother refers to my husband" to resume the parallel statements of detail about the scene and situation. "Marriage is the classic betrayal" seems to me a summarizing sentence, parallel to the thesis statement in the third sentence, if not a restatement of the thesis, and so on the same level of generality.

This ebbing and flowing also takes place when the topic sentence appears somewhere besides the beginning of the paragraph, too, as it often does:

I came away from the zoo with something, a piece of news about myself: I am coded, somehow, for otters and beavers.

I exhibit instinctive behavior in their presence, when they are displayed close at hand behind glass, simultaneously below water and at the surface.

I have receptors for this display.

Beavers and otters possess a "release" for me, in the terminology of ethology, and the releasing was my experience.

What was released?

Behavior.

What behavior

Standing,
swiveling
flabbergasted,
feeling
exultation and
a rush of
friendship.

I could not, as the result of the transaction, tell you anything more about beavers and otters than you already know.

I learned nothing new about them.

Only about me, and I suspect also about you, maybe about human beings at large:

We are endowed with genes which code out our reactions to beavers and otters, maybe our reaction to each other as well.

We are stamped with stereotyped, unalterable patterns of response, ready to be released.

And the behavior released in us, by such confrontations, is essentially, a surprised affection.

> It is compulsory behavior and we can avoid it only by straining with the full power of our conscious minds, making up excuses all the way.

Left to ourselves, mechanistic and autonomic, we hanker for friends.

I read this last sentence as the thesis statement, what the whole paragraph has been leading up to, although it's also possible to read it as a conclusion to the paragraph, parallel to the opening statement, a second thesis statement. Or it's possible to read it as still more particular than "It is compulsory behavior." What matters is the complexity and layers of the movement, the possibilities of parallelism in the first part of the paragraph and then the climaxing of that parallelism in the final statement.

A second way of viewing the internal operations of paragraphs uses a modified "slotting" system borrowed from linguistics, a kind of grammar of structure. The sentences within paragraphs can be understood as performing these logical functions:

(T):   stating a thesis, topic, or theme

(R):   restating the theme, refining, restricting it

(I):   illustrating the theme or thesis, giving examples of it

(A):   analyzing the thesis or the examples

(C):   concluding, closing

Transitional words typically indicate the movement from one slot to another, or are implicit in that movement. *R*s are often introduced with "that is" or "in other words"; *I*s with "for instance" or "for example"; *C*s with "thus" or "in conclusion."

These slots don't necessarily have to come in this order, although they often do. TRIAC is a natural progression: stating an idea, modifying it, illustrating it, and then analyzing the illustration. But a paragraph can also come in other orders: IAC, IRT, AT, TAC. TRIAC describes a grammar of structure that can be used to generate an infinite number of structural "sentences," a logic for organization that corresponds to the logic of thinking about a generalization.

Paragraphs don't have to have all of these slots at all. They may just be statements of theme to be illustrated or analyzed or restricted by other paragraphs in an organically developing bloc.

Here's the Didion paragraph again, with the slots or logical movements labeled:

(*T*) I am home for my daughter's first birthday.

[A statement of the general topic or theme; not a thesis but an announcement of an area of development.]

(*R*) By home I do not mean the house in Los Angeles where my husband and I and the baby live, but the place where my family is, in the Central Valley of California.

[That theme now restated, refined, restricted.]

(*R*) It is a vital, although troublesome distinction.

[Further refinement.]

(*I*) My husband likes my family but is uneasy in their house, because once there I fall into their ways, which are difficult, oblique, deliberately inarticulate, not my husband's ways.

[The next few sentences are the move to concrete example and illustration, the central strategy of Didion's style.]

(*I*) We live in dusty houses ("D-U-S-T," he once wrote with his finger on surfaces all over the house, but no one noticed it) filled with mementos quite without value to him (what could the Canton dessert plates mean to him? how could he have known about the assay scales, why should he care if he did know?), and we appear to talk exclusively about people we know who have been booked on drunk-driving charges, and about property, particularly about property, land, price per acre and C-2 zoning and assessments and freeway access.

(*I*) My brother does not understand my husband's inability to perceive the advantage in the rather common real-estate transaction known as "sale-leaseback," and my husband in turn does not understand why so many of the people he hears about in my father's house have recently been committed to mental hospitals or booked on drunk-driving charges.

(*I*) Nor does he understand that when we talk about sale-leasebacks and right-of-way condemnations we are talking in code about the things we like best, the yellow fields and the cottonwoods and the rivers rising and falling and the mountain roads closing when the heavy snow comes in.

>(*I*) We miss each other's points, have another drink and regard the fire.

>(*I*) My brother refers to my husband, in his presence, as "Joan's husband."

(*C*) Marriage is the classic betrayal.

[This could be interpreted as an analysis of the previous parallel sentences of the details. It might also be seen as a restatement of the opening theme in new terms drawn from the examples. For me it has the rhythmic and conceptual effect of climax, of closure.]

And the Thomas paragraph:

(*T*) I came away from the zoo with something, a piece of news about myself: I am coded, somehow, for otters and beavers.

[The theme announced.]

>(*R*) I exhibit instinctive behavior in their presence, when they are displayed close at hand behind glass, simultaneously below water and at the surface.

>(*R* becoming *A*) I have receptors for this display.

[Thomas is rephrasing in more particular terms his initial statement; as the rephrasing continues in the three parallel sentences here, he begins his analysis.]

(*A*) Beavers and otters possess a "release" for me, in the terminology of ethology, and the releasing was my experience.

[I see all that follows until the end as analysis.]

(*A*) What was released?

Behavior.

(*A*) What behavior?

Standing, swiveling flabbergasted, feeling exultation and a rush of friendship.

(*A*) I could not, as the result of the transaction, tell you anything more about beavers and otters than you already know.

(*A*) I learned nothing new about them.

(*A*) Only about me, and I suspect also about you, maybe about human beings at large:

(*A*) We are endowed with genes which code out our reactions to beavers and otters, maybe our reaction to each other as well.

(*A*) We are stamped with stereotyped, unalterable patterns of response, ready to be released.

(*A*) And the behavior released in us, by such confrontations, is, essentially, a surprised affection.

(*A*) It is compulsory behavior and we can avoid it only by straining with the full power of our conscious minds, making up excuses all the way.

(*T/C*) Left to ourselves, mechanistic and autonomic, we hanker for friends.

[Clearly this has the rhythm status of a conclusion, but again, I see it, too, as the thesis, the particular idea, that Thomas has been leading up to.]

''TRIACING'' A WHOLE ESSAY

*T*his slotting system can also be applied to whole essays, paragraphs or parts of paragraphs now occupying each slot. An essay can be read as a paragraph writ large, developing a central idea by means of these same logical functions:

THE TUCSON ZOO

Topic—
Thesis—
Theme

Science gets most of its information by the process of reductionism, exploring the details, then the details of the details, until all the smallest bits of the structure, or the smallest parts of the mechanism, are laid out for counting and scrutiny. Only when this is done can the investigation be extended to encompass the whole organism or the entire system. So we say.

But—But really—But in fact

Restriction,
Reversal
(new topic)

Illustration

Sometimes it seems that we take a loss, working this way. Much of today's public anxiety about science is the apprehension that we may forever be overlooking the whole by an endless, obsessive preoccupation with the parts. [*for instance*] I had a brief personal experience of this misgiving one afternoon in Tucson, where I had time on my hands and visited the zoo, just outside the city. The designers there have cut a deep pathway between two small artificial ponds, walled by clear glass, so when you stand in the center of the path you can look into the depths of each pool, and at the same time you can regard the surface. In one pool, on the right side of the path, is a family of otters; on the other side, a family of beavers. Within just a few feet from your face, on either side, beavers and otters are at play, underwater and on the surface, swimming toward your face and then away, more filled with life than any creatures I have ever seen before, in all my days. Except for the glass, you could reach across and touch them.

Furthermore—to continue

Illustration
—Analysis

I was transfixed. As I now recall it, there was only one sensation in my head: pure elation mixed with amazement at such perfection. Swept off my feet, I floated from one side to the other, swiveling my brain, staring astounded at the beavers, then at the otters. I could hear shouts across my corpus callosum, from one hemisphere to the other. [*What this means is*] I remember thinking, with what was left in charge of my consciousness, that I wanted no part of the science of beavers and otters; I wanted never to know how they performed their marvels; I wished for no news about the physiology of their breathing, the coordination of their muscles, their vision, their endocrine systems, their digestive tracts. I hoped never to have to think of them as collections of cells. All I asked for was the full hairy complexity, then in front of my eyes, of whole, intact beavers and otters in motion.

However—unfortunately—but

Analysis

It lasted, I regret to say, for only a few minutes, and then I was back in the late twentieth century, reductionist as ever, wondering about the details by force of habit, but not, this time, the details of otters and beavers. Instead, me. Something worth remembering had happened in my mind, I was certain of that; I would have put it somewhere in the brain stem; maybe this was my limbic system at work. I became a behavioral scientist, an experimental psychologist, an ethologist, and in the instant I lost all the wonder and the sense of being overwhelmed. I was flattened.

But—still—nonetheless—even so

Analysis

But I came away from the zoo with something, a piece of news about myself: I am coded, somehow, for otters and beavers. I exhibit instinctive behavior in their presence, when they are displayed close at hand behind glass, simultaneously below water and at the surface. I have receptors for this display. Beavers and otters possess a "release" for me, in the terminology of ethology, and the releasing was my experience. What was released? Behavior. What behavior? Standing, swiveling flabbergasted, feeling exultation and a rush of friendship. I could not, as the result of the transaction, tell you anything more about beavers and otters than you already know. I learned nothing new about them. Only about me, and I suspect also about you, maybe about human beings at large: we are endowed with genes which code out our reaction to beavers and otters, maybe our reaction to each other as well. We are stamped with stereotyped, unalterable patterns of response, ready to be released. And the behavior released in us, by such confrontations, is, essentially, a surprised affection. It is compulsory behavior and we can avoid it only by straining with the full power of our conscious minds, making up conscious excuses all the way. Left to ourselves, mechanistic and autonomic, we hanker for friends.

*Closure—
Refinement
of Thesis*

New Topic

Everyone says, stay away from ants. They have no lessons for us; they are crazy little instruments, inhuman, incapable of controlling themselves, lacking manners, lacking souls. When they are massed together, all touching, exchanging bits of information held in their jaws like memoranda, they become a single animal. Look out for that. It is a debasement, a loss of individuality, a violation of human nature, an unnatural act.

Indeed, in fact, and further

Analysis

Sometimes people argue this point of view seriously

and with deep thought. Be individuals, solitary and selfish, is the message. Altruism, a jargon word for what used to be called love, is worse than weakness, it is sin, a violation of nature. Be separate. Do not be a social animal. *But* this is a hard argument to make convincingly when you have to depend on language to make it. You have to print up leaflets or publish books and get them bought and sent around, you have to turn up on television and catch the attention of millions of other human beings all at once, and then you have to say to all of them, all at once, all collected and paying attention: be solitary; do not depend on each other. You can't do this and keep a straight face.

Restriction

On the contrary—in contrast—(that is)

Analysis

Maybe altruism is our most primitive attribute, out of reach, beyond our control. Or perhaps it is immediately at hand, waiting to be released, disguised now, in our kind of civilization, as affection or friendship or attachment. I don't see why it should be unreasonable for all human beings to have strands of DNA coiled up in chromosomes, coding out instincts for usefulness and helpfulness. Usefulness may turn out to be the hardest test of fitness for survival, more important than aggression, more effective, in the long run, than grabbiness. If this is the sort of information biological science holds for the future, applying to us as well as to ants, then I am all for science.

Thesis

Most of all (and further)

Question

One thing I'd like to know most of all: when those ants have made the Hill, and are all there, touching and exchanging, and the whole mass begins to behave like a single huge creature, and *thinks*, what on earth is that thought? And while you're at it, I'd like to know a second thing: when it happens, does any single ant know about it? Does his hair stand on end?

What labels to use and where to put them are matters of interpretation. You might put the first *A* earlier or later or imagine the sequence differently. Sometimes the shift from slot to slot seems to take place within a paragraph, as in the second paragraph here, when Thomas begins his illustration; other times the shifts seem to take place across paragraphs. The important point is that the structure of this essay—of any essay—depends on certain intellectual functions and that these functions can come in any number of sequences.

Notice that the *T* slot can appear more than once, and usually needs to in a longer pierce of discourse. Without that repetition of theme we lose track of the focusing idea of a piece of writing, the relationship of the parts. Notice, too, that the *C* slot can come before the end of an essay, in this case signaling the end of a bloc of paragraphs.

Just as authors are distinguished by the styles of their sentences—their rhythms and characteristic modifiers—they are also distinguished by structural or organizational styles, both within and across paragraphs. In most of her essays Didion tends to rely on *I* slots to carry the theme. After the brief sentences of thesis and restriction in the opening two paragraphs of "On Going Home," for example, the essay becomes a series of illustrations with little commentary of any sort. There isn't even an explicit conclusion per se but another dramatized image implicitly expressing her point—which is that definite conclusions aren't possible anymore. Thomas's structural style, in contrast, depends on the reversal of initial statements of theme and doesn't usually rely on extended illustrations. There are more *A*'s in Thomas than in Didion, within paragraphs and across blocs of paragraphs.

Of course, after a while slotting and analyzing like this starts looking silly, all these labels and letters like defense acronyms. This kind of analysis doesn't solve anything finally, or very much. The key thing is what goes inside the slots, the content.

TRIAC has three advantages over the five-paragraph theme or any other formula: (1) It's flexible, suggesting a set of possibilities for an infinite number of combinations. (2) It suggests operations, not just piles of things, helping writers understand what writers do, the kinds of intellectual moves they make (restricting, illustrating, etc.). (3) It helps explain something about the inner coherence of a piece, how the pieces are logically and expositionally related.

At the end of this chapter I'm including a student imitation of the structure of "The Tucson Zoo" by the writer of the Yaquina Bay dock essay in the second chapter. Notice how Roy has taken the exact TRIAC-ing scheme of the essay, even some of its transitions, and inserted his own content. In this case, as an exercise, form has come first, its movement and direction forcing the material into a certain shape.

AROUSAL AND FULFILLMENT

"*F*orm is an arousing and fulfillment of desires," Kenneth Burke says in *Counter-Statement*. "A work has form insofar as one part of it leads a reader to anticipate another part, to be gratified by the sequence."

This is the principle of form implicit in the movement of paragraphs as I've been describing them. If I say I'm going to talk about three things and only talk about two, I've disappointed the reader. I've not honored the implicit promise I've made at the beginning. If I state an argument and then don't go on to substantiate it, back it up, I've also let the reader down. An argument arouses the expectation of support, just as "Once upon a time" inevitably arouses "And then what happened? And then what?"

Burke also categorizes the basic kinds of patterns or sequences it is possible for a piece of writing—or music, or art, or architecture—to have. Four of these are useful for us.

Syllogistic form: a logical movement from *A* to *B* to *C*. If *A* is true, then *B* follows. An argument. A proof.

❏ *Qualitative form*: The presence of one quality prepares us for another quality. A dark and somber mood prepares us for crisis or struggle. One mood or feeling or atmosphere leads to the next, a feeling of satisfaction naturally preparing us for its frustration or destruction, highs leading to lows, and so on. Free associations.

❏ *Repetitive form*: A succession of images, illustrations, examples, details to elaborate or demonstrate an idea. The thesis-illustration pattern of the standard freshmen theme is repetitive in nature. "Repetitive form, the restatement of a theme by new details, is basic to any work of art, or to any other kind of orientation, for that matter. It is our only method for 'talking on the subject.' "

❏ *Conventional form*: An awareness of form as form, form signaling to us that the author is following a certain format. A sonnet. A funeral oration or graduation speech. The five-paragraph theme. Certain memo formats within companies. Whenever we call attention to the fact that we are deliberately and knowingly jumping through prescribed hoops jumped through by generations of predecessors—following tradition— we are engaged in conventions. This can be good or bad, effective or ineffective. That depends on whether or not the writer is in control of those conventions or just going through the motions; whether the reader has consented to that act of following conventions, whether the situation demands it, or whether the writer is rehearsing some tired set of conventions not necessary and not consented to.

It's possible for one work to have elements of all of these patterns. "The Tucson Zoo" mixes the syllogistic and the qualitative: the syllogistic in Thomas's thinking aloud about what the experience means, his analysis; the qualitative in the emotional progression from joy in the beavers and otters to the experience of flattening to the experience of recovery and insight. "On Going Home" is both repetitive and qualitative: a mood of uneasiness, nostalgia, longing reinforced by clusters of images and details.

Like the theory of paragraphing and slotting and logical relationships I've offered, Burke's general notion of form is significant for what it doesn't say. Burke doesn't say that you have to write any particular piece in any particular order. His interest is in the underlying logic and experience of form, not in prescriptions made out of the fear of chaos and sloppiness.

He leads you to ask some functional questions as you read a piece of writing or start revising a piece of your own: What do I expect to happen next? What have I been led to believe will follow? What do I need to happen next? What's missing? What's required? Where have my expectations been fulfilled, frustrated? Where am I lost?

CONCRETENESS

*D*etails are the content that gives shape to form. Without examples, demonstrations, analysis, there wouldn't be anything to have a form or shape, just a list of two or three propositions, the main points on an outline. Why isn't it effective to turn in an outline instead of the whole paper and be done with it? Because the fundamental expectation of form is for elaboration and support. You say it's so, but is it true? You say you know this, but do you really? You say you feel this, but what do you mean?

The ebbing and flowing of sentences beneath a paragraph, and all the ebbing and flowing of a whole essay—all those interrelationships— come from the need for depth and detail and real experience. We need to *show*, not just *tell*.

One use of the TRIACing scheme is to reveal quickly and graphically the absence of *I*s and *A*s in student writing, essaywide and within paragraphs. Not every paragraph needs all the slots, and the slots don't have to come in a certain order. But finally paragraphs and themes need a good number of *I*s and *A*s or they lack development.

Diagram paragraphs, too, showing their ebbs and flows, or the absence of ebbs and flows. If there isn't that movement, there isn't enough thinking:

(T) This change in the role that family plays might be attributed to the "me" generation.

[Easy to say. A truism. We're waiting to see the proof, the illustration.]

(R) In general people are very selfish today.

[A restatement, a degree more particular. But we're still waiting.]

(I) The other week a boy I had been seeing said, "Don't try to tie me down. I'm not going to commit to one girl."

[Ah! Not a great or original example, but at least there is one. There's a connection, not just a truism.]

(A) That statement really didn't phase me, his reasoning behind it did.

[Not just the example, then, but some analysis of it, some thinking about it. The paragraph is moving farther and farther to the right, which is to say, it's getting more and more particular, extended, and so better and better.]

(*A*) The relationship worked well for him.

(*A*) It was convenient.

(*A*) I would always be there if he needed a date, but if something came his way he was ready.

[Three parallel statements of analysis, an explanation of why the reasoning "phased" the writer.]

(*A*) I asked around to see what other people thought of this idea.

[Jumping back out to generalize, think through what's problematic about the boyfriend's reasoning].

(*A*) The general consensus was that this worked well with everyone.

[The results of her questioning, which complicate her thesis, are at odds with it. The paragraph is getting richer, more layered, and yet it's all holding together, all subordinate to the opening thesis about selfishness.]

(*C/T*) How can marriage work if everyone is always worrying that they might be missing out on something better?

[An argument with the consensus, which reinforces and clarifies again why she is fazed by her boyfriend. More particular than the opening generalization about the "me generation" but in a sense the real thesis of the paragraph. Also a kind of conclusion.]

versus:

(*T*) The home life in families headed by only one parent is just as strong or stronger than in a family headed by two because the family becomes closer and is more willing to work out problems when they arise.

[A statement of theme arousing the expectation—or the hope, at least— of some demonstration and example.]

The Shape of Content 103

(*T*) This, in turn, is good for the child because the child has had this influence and will carry it on to his/her family.

[You might be tempted to label this an *A* because of "in turn," but on a second reading it's clear that this is really an assertion of another theme, related to the first but logically distinct. It's perhaps a degree more detailed than the first, but only very slightly. What we're missing is the illustration and analysis of the previous statement.]

(*T*) Children also learn a better sense of independence, which makes them more ready for the "real world."

[More of the same. Assertions without development. And note the connective "also." We have three sentences strung together here, not sequenced.]

(*T*) A lot more families today are headed by parents who both work.

[A new thesis entirely, not a subthesis. We've moved from single-parent homes to "latch-key" homes. This could be a new paragraph, in fact, assuming there were examples—*I* slots—to develop the points.]

(*T/A*) It would lead one to think that this would be detrimental to the family.

[Some analysis, some "if/then" thinking going on, so some genuine movement. But again only slight.]

(*T/A*) But actually the quality of time spent together is much better than the length.

[The same as the previous statement.]

(*T*) Parents who are willing to work on their family life make sure that the quality of time spent with their family is high.

[Another big, thesis statement—the third thesis—which follows from this last generalization but really introduces an entirely new line of thought to be developed.]

What's obvious is that the first paragraph is more developed. It moves back and forth underneath a main statement: develops through analysis and illustration a single point. The second is a collection of separate statements that could in fact be topic sentences for separate paragraphs or paragraph blocs. It's virtually flush left. Each statement moves on to the next without *Is* and *As*. There's no obvious transition or sequence from one to the next, other than "also," as in "and here's another point." In the end, even though this second paragraph is actually longer than the first, it says much less.

In Chapter 2 we talked about issues of authenticity and voices in pieces of writing. They are very much connected to concreteness. We buy something if it's demonstrated, brought down to earth. And that usually means the writer's either showing research and statistics or acknowledging the connection between the generalization she is making and her own real experience in the world.

The ebbing and flowing, and the slotting, in short, are more ways of representing what we've been talking about throughout the book.

DICTATING PICTURES

*I*n "Why I Write," Joan Didion describes the relationship between form and content in these terms:

> The arrangement of the words matters, and the arrangement you want can be found in the picture in your mind. The picture dictates the arrangement. The picture dictates whether this will be a sentence with or without clauses, a sentence that ends hard or a dying-fall sentence, long or short, active or passive. The picture tells you how to arrange the words and the arrangement of the words tells you, or tells me, what's going on in the picture. Nota bene:
> It tells you.
> You don't tell it.

This may seem too philosophical and creative-writerly to apply to your own day-to-day writing, all well and good for someone like Joan Didion but not relevant to the ordinary people of the world. But it is relevant. Feigned forms, mechanical forms never work, especially for inexperienced writers. All you know is all you know, and no amount of hoop jumping or formula following is going to disguise that finally, at least most of the time. You might as well come clean. If you only have two real points, write a *four*-paragraph theme. And while you're at it, why not trying ending with a question?

·········· S KETCHBOOK

✐ Take an essay, article, or part of a chapter or report you are currently reading and outline its structure using TRIAC. You can use "On Going Home," for example. What are the transitions between sections? Do the paragraphs form into blocs and how are those pieces related? Does the outlining expose any weaknesses? Reveal any structures worth imitating?

Could the prose be paragraphed differently? What would be the effect of those new indentations?

REVISION

✐ Revise the first or second practice piece using the discussion in this chapter. You might want to TRIAC the piece first, determine what's missing or repetitive. Focus both on transitions and development: Can readers move easily from one part to another? Is each idea adequately developed? Is it possible, too, to make the structure less mechanical and obvious without sacrificing coherence? Are there other, more effective ways to paragraph? Is there a workable structure in the original free-writing? If the piece already seems coherent, if it works as is, what makes it work?

You might even try to rewrite one of the practice pieces as a structural imitation of "The Tucson Zoo," the way Roy has in "Profit for Whom?" putting your own content into Thomas's structure.

Profit for Whom?

Fishery resources are being managed for the maximum benefit of fishery user groups. That's a reasonable practice, wholly in keeping with the philosophy that it is a function of government to assist hard-working entrepreneurs in making a profit from their productivity, and to manage natural resources so they keep producing. It's good for the economy, and good for the country. It helps keep America strong. And besides, it's the public and the users who provide the money for resource management.

But it's not always a good idea, managing a resource for maximum profit. This past summer there was research conducted by Japanese fishing vessels, with the cooperation of U.S. agencies and scientists, exploring for squid a few miles off our coast. Their intent was to determine if there were enough squid to make it profitable to fish for them. The research was not a success, not necessarily because of a low abundance of squid, but for reasons of ocean conditions at that particular time, so that the scientists did not find enough squid in their predetermined search pattern. The fishermen will be back to try it again, I am sure.

Time after time, scientists and government agencies are willing to cooperate with fishermen in exploiting yet another resource at the edge of our continental shelf without determining what ecological impact it would have on other marine species. These explorers were looking for squid, not relationships between squid and other species. If the squid are removed, then the fish populations utilizing those squid as food may also be reduced. The scientists know that. It's just another intrusion of capitalism: profit-seeking imposed on a natural system that has its definition of profit based on millions of years of evolution.

The world is full of examples of human overuse. From the forests of Lebanon to the dodo bird to the American bison to the California sardines, we have a long history of exploiting resources to the point of diminishing returns, when there is no longer enough of the resource to make exploitation worthwhile. Until it is no longer profitable.

But there may be a point of no return. There may be a point of balance where the rest of life on earth can no longer sustain human overuse. The trouble is, we have no idea where that point might be, or how soon we will be there.

Sea urchins are wonderfully strange creatures, purple pincushions twice the size of your fist sliding along a reef, grazing the algae like herds of little underwater buffalo, spines all a-bristle to protect them from piscivorous carnivores. Sea otters like to eat them, need them, even, since the urchins are a staple of the otter diet. Likewise, the algae need the otters, otherwise the urchins would multiply and graze the algae right off the reef. Then the fish would suffer for lack of shelter, and so would the tiny invertebrates that cling to the algae, providing food for the fish.

People, too, like to eat urchins, especially the Japanese, who pay dearly for the privilege of eating the urchin gonads that weigh half as much as the entire urchin. This choice of delicacies presents a wonderful opportunity for American entrepreneurs, those independent-minded souls who need to be their own boss. Fine, strong boats are built, aluminum-hulled, broad-beamed craft that can handle ocean waves and bumps against rocks, and can serve as a diving platform for urchin fishermen who gather urchins into large baskets to be winched to the surface. There is a lot of money to be made here.

Money, and exchange, is the driving force behind this exploitation. But where lies the wisdom in learning to utilize every possible plant and animal population in the ocean, taking up to half of each, as past population dynamics theory suggests is possible? The ultimate result will be that there will be only half as much life in the ocean as there was before.

I don't know if it is possible for humans to slow this mad destruction, this dependence on natural resources, this taking of more than we need. Are we like the urchins? Will we graze ourselves right off the reef?

....

5

THE SECRET OF SYNTAX

It seemed as though every rule he honestly tried to discover with them and learn with them was so full of exceptions and contradictions and qualifications and confusions that he wished he'd never come across the rule in the first place . . . what he really thought was that the rule was pasted on to the writing after the writing was all done. It was post hoc, after the fact, instead of prior to the fact. And he became convinced that all the writers the students were supposed to mimic wrote without rules, putting down whatever sounded right, then going back to see if it still sounded right and changing it if it didn't. There were some who apparently wrote with calculating premeditation because that's the way their product looked. But that seemed to him to be a very poor way to look.

—Robert Pirsig, *Zen and the Art of Motorcycle Maintenance*

*F*ree/style also depends on syntax—not just the words you use but the order you put them in. As you write and revise, you're always rephrasing and rearranging, smoothing out some sentences to make them more direct, blending others together to avoid sounding choppy. It doesn't matter whether you say "bought" instead of "purchased" if you arrange those words in an awkward order. The underlying structure of sentences is the key to a natural-sounding style.

There are two important tricks here, and they go together. Say things directly, the subject first and then what the subject is doing. Then trail the modifiers, putting the modifying phrases at the end of the straightforward declarations, expanding and contracting them, adjusting their rhythm as you need to, creating texture, refining with detail.

THE PROBLEM OF NOMINALIZATION

*O*ne of the root problems of writing we perceive as bad or insincere is nominalization. A nominalization is a concrete subject-verb declaration that's been translated into an abstract noun phrase:

> When I recall my childhood I often think with delight of treasured experiences.

becomes

> Recalling childhood memories often brings delight and a recollection of treasured experiences.

The second version is what the writer turned in. The first is my translation of it back into a more direct and straightforward structure. What I've done is remove the nominalizations. "Recalling childhood memories" is really a noun phrase based on the direct subject-verb statement "I recall." "Recollection" is a nominalization based on "I recollect." The sentence I've written around these two declarations isn't great even so, but it seems to me noticeably better.

Or here's a typical memo I've just received from one of the administrators at my university:

The authorization to offer MA/MS degrees in Scientific and Technical Communication makes it necessary to designate a director for that program.

Who in the world did this "authorization," anyway? And who is going to designate a director? The dean himself, of course, along with an advisory committee. Why not something like this, then:

Now that the university has authorized the new degree in Scientific and Technical Communication, we need to designate a director.

There's still some deanlike diction here—"authorized" and "designate"—and still some vagueness about who exactly is doing what—the "we." But do you hear the difference?

Notice how nominalization is related to diction but is not the same thing. A word like "authorization" is stuffy and abstract and so like many of the words we talked about in Chapter 3. But it's also more than that. It's a determiner of word order, an abstracter of syntax.

Underneath every abstract phrase is an implicit subject-verb statement, someone or something *doing* something. Just like that. The subject of the statement is clear, and it's clear that the subject is performing some action in the world. Not:

Nominalization is a bad thing. *or* Nominalization should be avoided at all costs.

but

Students shouldn't nominalize. *or* If you want to make your prose style clear, use concrete subjects and concrete verbs.

Those direct and simpler sentences are the basis of a good style. It's better just to say it, in short. Nominalization doesn't sound natural. It's as if you've had to stop and think about what you're going to say instead of just saying it. You're putting up a front, translating.

And yet rhythmically the demand for directness may seem counterintuitive at first, since there is also a demand in good writing to be sophisticated and complicated and for the writing to "flow" in some way. You don't want to be caught being simple minded or sounding uneducated. If you write nothing but simple and direct sentences, won't the writing sound primer-style and elementary? It's that question, that impulse, that leads so many students to circumlocutions and round-aboutness and ultimately to sentences like these, from a recent master's thesis I had to read:

> Establishing a primary disease prevention program with the involve-ment of the entire population is an important cancer control strategy in the promotion of health and the prevention of disease.

> While experimentation can establish the causal association of a factor with a disease more conclusively than observation, observational studies have provided and continue to provide the major contribution to our understanding of many diseases.

> Progress in any health program depends on evaluation of the result of previous efforts. Thus, in order to measure an event, establishing an ideal standard in a program is necessary.

Yes, you want to be sophisticated and authoritative when you write, but this isn't how you do it. Multiply these sentences by hundreds over nearly fifty pages, and what you have is vague, abstract, terribly difficult reading. There's no one home in this writing. The writer's decision to nominalize is based on a decision or an instinct (misguided) about voice. When you nominalize you sound academic, you sound more like you're writing a master's thesis. And finally you end up writing unread-able prose.

Here are the nominalizations in those three passages:

> Establishing *versus* I establish, the U.N. establishes, the World Health Organization establishes or should establish, scientists establish or should establish (*somebody* establishes)

> Prevention *versus* We prevent, medicine prevents, the World Health Organization should try to prevent (*somebody* prevents, or tries to)

involvement
promotion
experimentation
association
observation
contribution

understanding
progress
evaluation
establishing

Most nominalizations are either "-tion" words, Latinate and scientific sounding, or "-ing" words. Each can be translated back into some subject-verb statement. The central conceptual problem of this essay was who the writer ultimately thought was responsible for the actions she was recommending. Should the World Health Organization take charge? Should individual countries? Should the United States? Money is involved here, structural changes. But it turned out that the writer wasn't sure who should take responsibility, and that uncertainty was reflected in these sentences. Style reflects and embodies content.

After several revisions and some genuine rethinking of her project, she came up with these polished versions:

To help prevent cancer, developing countries should establish a primary disease prevention program that involves the entire population.

[Notice that she's kept some of the nominalization here—"disease prevention program." That's a technical phrase in this field, and in the end it saves time and space just to use it. Notice, too, that eliminating the nominalization also entails cutting out words and condensing in general.]

Experimentation is the best way to establish the cause of a disease, but scientists and other researchers can also learn a great deal simply from observing the disease as it actually happens in a community.

[Again, "experimentation" seems to work here, even though it's a nominalization. The rest of the sentence, though, depends on making "scientists and other researchers" the subject. In the process of defusing the nominals, the writer has also moved the sentence a little more toward the informal.]

Agencies need to evaluate their health programs if they hope to improve them. And to measure progress effectively, they need to establish an ideal standard.

By concrete subjects and concrete verbs, I don't necessarily mean human subjects or physical actions. Ideas can function as subjects and intellectual operations can function as verbs. Which is to say that these sentences are still pretty abstract and generalized. They have to be, given the subject matter. What makes them better than the originals is that these abstractions now occupy direct slots, are now set up in direct relationships. The result is that we can read and understand the ideas more quickly. The thing or agency doing the action is stated right away, and then immediately the action is specified, spelled out. We know the main logical relationship, who is responsible for what. It also just takes less time to transact the business of a sentence that way, uses fewer words. Somehow we are coded to apprehend information in terms of subject-verb relationships. We just tend to think that way, and when those relationships are suspended, we get more easily lost or irritated.

In "Politics and the English Language," George Orwell demonstrates the power of directness by "translating" a passage from Ecclesiastes into what he calls "modern English."

> I returned and saw under the sun, that the race is not to the swift, nor the battle to the strong, neither yet bread to the wise, not yet riches to men of understanding, nor yet favor to men of skill; but time and chance happeneth to them all.

> Objective consideration of contemporary phenomena compels the conclusion that success or failure in competitive activities exhibits no tendency to be commensurate with innate capacity, but that a considerable element of the unpredictable must invariably be taken into account.

There's lots going on in this passage besides nominalization: what Orwell earlier in the essay identifies as "dying metaphors," "operators or verbal false limbs," "pretentious diction," "meaningless words." But nominalization is at the source. These other problems are connected to it, reflected by it, maybe even caused by it, since when you start nominalizing you're almost forced to inflate your diction and write in passive voice. To put this another way, when you decide to write in a deliberately academic and inflated voice, you naturally start nominalizing. It's the engine that drives this kind of prose.

It's easy to do the same kind of thing to a paragraph from "The Tucson Zoo," and in ruining it see its real strength:

> I was transfixed. As I now recall it, there was only one sensation in my head: pure elation mixed with amazement at such perfection. Swept off

The Secret of Syntax   115

my feet, I floated from one side to the other, swiveling my brain, staring astounded at the beavers, then at the otters. I could hear shouts across my corpus callosum, from one hemisphere to the other. I remember thinking, with what was left in charge of my consciousness, that I wanted no part of the science of beavers and otters; I wanted never to know how they performed their marvels; I wished for now news about the physiology of their breathing, the coordination of their muscles, their vision, their endocrine systems, their digestive tracts. I hoped never to have to think of them as collections of cells. All I asked for was the full hairy complexity, then in front of my eyes, of whole, intact beavers and otters in motion.

My recollection is that amazement and perfection overwhelmed and transfixed me. Astonishment at the sight of the beavers and otters created a movement back and forth from the hemispheres of my brain, across the corpus callosum. My memory is that the desire to understand the physiology of their breathing and the structure of their endocrine system suddenly evaporated. Contemplation of cell structure was no longer relevant or important. My desire for the full, hairy complexity of whole, intact beavers and otters.

The problem in the second version is that no one is present, nothing intact or in motion, either beavers or otters, or Thomas himself. There's no hairy complexity. With the original subject-verb pattern gone, the scientific jargon overwhelms the prose and there's only the disembodied voice of "recollections" and "astonishment."

But the original Thomas passage also emphasizes how nominalization has to do with the word order and not just word choice. Thomas uses "I" here, but he also uses some sophisticated terms, some jargon: "corpus callosum" and "endocrine systems." He does this on purpose. It's part of the tension he wants to create, a tension between the immediacy of his own experience and the abstractness of the scientific terminology he uses as a researcher himself. Good, concrete, subject-verb patterns can have any words put into them, scientific, jargon-filled, bureaucratic even. You don't have to use "I" or be informal.

Which is to say that this structure is the key to good prose across genre and discipline lines, as applicable to a technical report as to a personal essay.

Notice, too, that Thomas uses nominalizations when they suit him ("there was only one sensation," for example). Mechanically in-

sisting on subject-verb sentences in every case would make the prose
rote and mechanical. Sometimes the nominalization seems right, comes
to you. (The last two sentences I wrote depend on nominalization, for
example: "Insisting" and "nominalization.") I'm sure that Thomas
doesn't give it a thought, doesn't sit down and think, well, I can't use
that phrase because it's a nominalization, or, I better use the subject-
verb form here. He just writes. My point is that Thomas's prose doesn't
depend on nominalizations. It doesn't issue from the decisions about
voice that nominalizations always reflect but instead is grounded in
Thomas's courage to say what he thinks and feels head on: "I could
hear," "I remember thinking," "I wanted never to know."

Back to the question I raised earlier, then. If you begin your
sentences with the subject and then go right to the verb, won't your
prose sound primer-style? There's false sophistication and true sophistication. Real flow and movement in prose isn't created through nominalization but through modifiers and variations on the basic structural
pattern of subject-verb. You put modifying phrases before and after it
(usually after, I'll show next), or in the middle. It's the simple subject-
verb sentence that carries or drives all good prose styles:

> I used to worry that computers would become so powerful and
> sophisticated as to take the place of human minds. The notion of Arti-
> ficial Intelligence used to scare me half to death. Already a large enough
> machine can do all sorts of intelligent things beyond our capacities:
> calculate in a split second the answers to mathematical problems requir-
> ing years for a human brain, draw accurate pictures from memory, even
> manufacture successions of sounds with a disarming resemblance to real
> music. Computers can translate textbooks, write dissertations of their
> own for doctorates, even speak in machine-tooled, inhuman phonemes
> any words read off from a printed page. They can communicate with one
> another, holding consultations and committee meetings of their own in
> networks around the earth.

The thing to notice about this passage for now—it's from another essay
by Thomas, "Out of the Corner of the Eye"—is that every sentence
begins with the subject and each subject is immediately followed by a
verb. But the movement isn't choppy or simplistic. Thomas is in no
danger of being mistaken for unsophisticated. The variety and flow is
created through modifying additions to that basic structure, here all at
the end (with the exception of the "already" in the third sentence). The

colon indicates that relationship in the third sentence: first the general statement, clear and subject-verb, then the unpacking of it in a series of parallel verb phrases. The last sentence has the same structure without the colon, a declaration followed by a modifying phrase. It's all built on the principle of straightforward saying, on subjects and verbs: Machines can do, Computers can translate, They can communicate. No nominalizations anywhere.

PASSIVE VOICE

*P*assive voice is often used by writers for all the reasons nominalizations are used. As in that last sentence. Not: "Writers often use passive voice and nominalization." That's active; the subject is stated first and is doing the action. In the passive version the real subject, the noun actually performing the action, is buried later in the sentence ("by writers") and the object of the action is made the subject ("Passive voice").

"The logger chainsawed the fir tree" is active voice; "the fir tree was chainsawed by the logger" is passive.

Often the subject is not just buried but implied, not there at all, as in part of Orwell's "translation": "A considerable element of the unpredictable must invariably be taken into account." Taken into account by whom? That's not said. There's no "taken into account by all concerned" or whatever. Similarly, "The fir tree was chainsawed" is less clumsy than the original passive voice, and it's even better at blurring responsibility for actions. No one's to blame here. Things just happened.

The problem with passive voice is like the problem with nominalization. It takes more words. It distances the actors from the actions of the sentence. It makes the language sound bureaucratic and vague.

It's not always bad, something to avoid self-consciously and at all costs. Sometimes passive constructions are necessary in the rhythm of the sentence or to establish coherence among sentences. Sometimes who or what is responsible for the action of the sentence isn't relevant or important. I slipped into a natural or readable passive construction in explaining the passive: "The subject is stated first and is doing the action . . . the real subject is buried in the sentence . . . the object is made the subject." My emphasis in this part of the paragraph is on "subjects" and "objects," not on the writers of sentences like that.

THE CUMULATIVE SENTENCE

Now the second part of the secret. Professional, published writers put their modifiers *at the end* of their sentences two thirds of the time. They begin with a straightforward declaration, free of nominalization. Then, instead of ending with a period, they change the period to a comma and start adding modifiers, refining and extending the main statement, clarifying it, adding detail to it, the subordinate phrases and clauses unpacking the initial statement by degrees, showing its parts and qualities, its layers:

> I used to park my car on a hill and sit silently observant, listening to the talk ringing out from neighbor to neighbor, seeing the inhabitants drowsing in their doorways, taking it all in with nostalgia—the sage smell of the wind, the sunlight without time, the village without destiny.

> —*Loren Eiseley*

Logically the sentence is over by "and sit silently observant." We know the actor and the action. The sentence could end there and we'd have a complete thought, a grammatical whole. The modifying phrases are subordinate to it, contained in it. They don't extend the action or idea any further—they don't add—but instead elaborate, focus:

I used to park my car on a hill and sit silently observant,

listening to the talk ringing out from neighbor to neighbor, (VC)

seeing the inhabitants drowsing in their doorways,   (VC)

taking it all in with nostalgia—   (VC)

the sage smell of the wind,   (NC)

the sunlight without time,   (NC)

the village without destiny.   (NC)

I'll explain the labeling in a minute. For now all I want you to see is the movement, the ebbing and flowing of the modifying phrases underneath the main sentence. I've tried to represent this movement by indenting phrases further to the right the more detailed they are, the more concrete or extended. The phrases unfold. They float freely underneath: are all "free modifiers," not directly attached to anything other than the initial statement itself, free to come in whatever order occurs to the writer at the moment. They are only loosely related to one another, each successive phrase either parallel to what preceded it or progressively more detailed, a further step in the elaboration, another level. We could put a period after any level of modification and have a complete sentence grammatically.

It's real writers who rely on this kind of sentence. The "cumulative" sentence—or the "loose" sentence—is the stock in trade of contemporary prose style:

There were black Saturdays now and then

    when Maria and Miranda sat ready, (SC)

        hats in hand, (ABS)

        curly hair plastered down and slicked behind their ears, (ABS)

        their stiffly-pleated navy-blue skirts spread out around them, (ABS)

    waiting with their hearts going down slowly into their high-topped laced-up black boots. (VC)

    —Katherine Anne Porter

The main clause describes the general sitting and waiting of Maria and Miranda, then each phrase describes a part of their bodies or clothing—hats, hair, skirt. The last phrase moves back out to describe their attitude as they wait.

I edged forward into a 45 degree hunker,

> my heels still resting against the ice-catching eyelets,   (ABS)

> my right hand now upon the gable.   (ABS)

> *—Roger Zelazny*

Zelazny first describes the hunker in general, then the two parts of the body—heels and hand—all in one sentence, one movement.

In the shoebox stuffed in an old nylon stocking sleeps the baby mouse I found in the meadow,

> where he trembled and shook beneath a stick still I caught him up by the tail and brought him in,   (SC)

> cradled in my head,   (AC)

> the whole body of him trembling,   (ABS)

>> his absurd whiskers sticking out like a cartoon mouse, (ABS)

>> his feet like small leaves,   (ABS)

>>> little lizard feet,   (NC)

>>> whitish and spread wide when he tried to struggle away,   (AC)

>>> wriggling like a miniscule puppy.   (VC)

> *—Theodore Roethke*

This is poetry, arranged here to indicate the cumulative movement. Defining the levels the way I have is finally impressionistic. Readers can disagree about what's subordinate to what. But it's obvious, for example, that "little lizard feet" is a more specific description of "feet" and so belongs underneath it and to the right—is contained in it. The sentence moves as a whole from the general to the increasingly particular.

Here are some examples from Didion and Thomas. First, some fairly short cumulatives from Didion:

We live in dusty houses,

 filled with mementos quite without value to him.   (AC)

The monuments are broken,

 overturned in the dry grass.   (AC)

We get along very well,

 veterans of a guerrilla war we never understood.   (NC)

The first two sentences here are slightly simplified from their original context, where they appear in the midst of other constructions.

He does not understand that when we talk about sale-leasebacks and right-of-way condemnations we are talking in code about the things we like best,

 the yellow fields and the cottonwoods and the rivers rising and falling and the mountain roads closing when the heavy snow comes in.   (NC)

Although the second phrase is fairly long, it is still one phrase. Notice that it repeats the main sentence in a sense. It explains what is meant by the sentence, as if an arrow or an equal sign exists over the comma.
 From Thomas:

Science gets most of its information by the process of reductionism,

 exploring the details,   (VC)

 then the details of the details,   (NC)

 until all the smallest bits of the structure, or the smallest parts of the mechanism, are laid out for counting and scrutiny.   (PP)

Within just a few feet from your face,   (PP)

on either side,   (PP)

beavers and otters are at play,

underwater and on the surface,   (AC)

swimming toward your face and then away,   (VC)

more filled with life than any creatures I have ever seen before,   (AC)

in all my days.   (PP)

Here in the second sentence there are two phrases before the main clause, though the main modification takes place after it. Notice how Thomas creates the effect of movement back and forth—imitating the motion of beavers and otters—by using cumulative modifiers in even, alternating rhythm.

I exhibit instinctive behavior in their presence,

when they are displayed close at hand behind glass,   (SC)

simultaneously below water and at the surface.   (PP)

Usefulness may turn out to be the hardest test of fitness for survival,

more important than aggression,   (AC)

more effective, in the long run, than grabbiness.   (AC)

In both these sentences Thomas manipulates the cumulative phrasing to create a brief, descriptive balance.

The trailing phrases, then, can be long or short, symmetrical or asymmetrical. By expanding and contracting them, arranging them in patterns of emphasis, a writer can create a variety of tones and voices. The movement is always simply from the general to the particular, like a camera zooming in. The details describe parts of the whole, general qualities or impressions of it, other things it is like.

THE PERIODIC SENTENCE

*I*n contrast, a periodic sentence:

> It comes as a great shock to discover that the country which is your birthplace and to which you owe your life and identity has not, in its whole system of reality, evolved any place for you.

> —*James Baldwin*

This sentence can't end anywhere but at the end. We can't put a period at "shock" or "country" or "has not." The structure and meaning isn't completed until the final word. It's suspended, unlike the cumulative, where the meaning is fixed right away and everything else is just a working out of the different corners or dimensions of what's already been said in general. Another:

> Natures that have much heart, and great and violent desires and perturbations, are not ripe for action till they have passed the meridian of their years.

> —*Francis Bacon*

Periodic sentences are fine things and contemporary prose depends on them, too. But it's the cumulative sentence that usually does the important stylistic work. It's the cumulative writers turn to when they want to emphasize or elaborate and intensify.

THE TERMINOLOGY

*I*t's important not to get too flummoxed or worried about this terminology, although it's not that hard to understand. You can write good cumulative sentences without knowing an absolute from a verb cluster. What's useful about the terminology is that it helps you see the great flexibility of this kind of sentence, and its underlying logic. It can also help you see what *to do* as a writer, since what grammar finally describes is a set of moves or operations, a set of intellectual actions.

Verb clusters (VC): modifying phrases clustered around an opening verb, usually an "-ing" word (or a participle)

seeing the inhabitants
taking it all in
wriggling like a puppy
swimming towards your face and then away

Verb clusters modify the subject of the main sentence or the preceding phrase ("I," the mouse, the beavers and otters, etc.).

Noun clusters (NC): modifying phrases clustered around a central noun

the sage *smell* of the wind
the *sunlight* without time
veterans of a guerrilla war
the yellow *fields* and the *cottonwoods* and the *rivers* rising and falling and the mountain *roads* closing when the snows come in.

Notice that noun clusters can contain adjectives, prepositional phrases, and other constructions. What makes them noun clusters is that these other modifiers are clustered around the noun—it's the noun that controls the phrase. This is particularly characteristic of Didion, who uses noun phrases for repetition, clarification, and emphasis, first stating the notion in the main clause and then rephrasing the idea once, sometimes twice, in another noun phrase.

It's a simple and very useful strategy, a way of quickly emphasizing or explaining an idea (as in this last phrase).

Adjective clusters (AC): a phrase centered on a controlling adjective or adjectives

whitish and *spread wide*
more filled with life
more important than aggression

The difference between adjectives in a noun cluster ("yellow fields") and adjectives in their own cluster is that adjective clusters modify a noun in the previous phrase or in the main sentence ("mouse," "beavers and otters," "usefulness"). They don't have their own noun (within the phrase): "life" is the object of a preposition, part of a phrase modifying the adjective; "aggression" is part of a comparative phrase controlled by "more important."

Prepositional phrases (PP):   any phrase beginning with a preposition (*with, in, to, at, from, like, under, over, below*)

on either side
in all my days

Subordinate clauses (SC):   any independent clause with a subordinating conjunction in front of it (*when, since, while, because, after, and so on*)

when Maria and Miranda sat ready
where he trembled and shook beneath a stick

When you remove the subordinating word from a clause like this, what you have is something that can stand as a complete sentence.

Relative clauses (RC):   similar to a subordinate clause except that the subordinating word is also the subject of the clause—a relative pronoun (*which, who, that*).

There aren't any examples of these in the sentences I've included. Somehow they're not as common.

Relative clauses sometimes sound a little awkward, *which* is maybe the reason writers don't rely on them too often.

"Which" is both the subject of the clause and the word that makes it subordinate to the main clause.

Absolute (ABS):   a verb cluster with its own noun.

This is the trickiest of the modifying phrases, and in some ways the slickest, since it frees you to create new subjects of modification at any level of the sentence. It frees you from logical dependence on the sub-ject of the main clause.

> my heels still resting against the ice-catching eyelets
> the whole body of him trembling

By itself, "resting against" is a verb cluster. "Trembling" is a verbal. Without the two nouns inserted in front of them, each would modify a noun in the preceding phrase or clause: "I" would be resting and "mouse" would be trembling. But the absolute allows the writer to specify a new noun at a new level of detail, to zero in on a part or dimension of the initial concept and make that the new center of the action: "heels resting," "body trembling." The noun doing the action is *in* the phrase.

Another way of understanding the absolute is to think of it as a deactivated sentence—a sentence where the verb has been deactivated, made into a verb*al*, an "-ing" or "-ed" form:

> My heels still rest*ed* against the ice-catching eyelets
> *becomes*
> my heels rest*ing*

> The whole body of him trembl*ed*
> *becomes*
> the whole body of him trembl*ing*.

If the implicit verb is a form of "to be," you just delete it.

> my right hand now upon the gable

is based implicitly on the sentence:

> My right hand *was* upon the gable.

> Their stiffly-pleated navy-blue skirts spread out around them

is a transformation of the complete sentence:

> Their stiffly-pleated navy-blue skirts *were* spread out around them.

Any sentence can be deactivated or converted in this way, its verbs made into verbals, its subject then freed up to float in the sentence, loosely subordinate to the main clause. It's a have-your-cake-and-eat-it-too construction, combining the advantages of complete sentences and modifying phrases.

This is the repertoire of modifiers writers have at their disposal, their battery or arsenal. There isn't anything else. This is the finite set—a "grammar" in the sense of a limited number of possible operations that can be used to generate an infinite number of patterns and combinations. Each kind of phrase carries logical and semantic possibilities, opportunities for meaning. Noun clusters, for example, tend to emphasize descriptive and spatial details; adjective clusters, general qualities; verb clusters (of course), dimensions of action; subordinate clauses, subordinate or causal or temporal relationships.

Writers tend to favor certain kinds of phrases over others. Some naturally favor noun modifiers and verb clusters; the styles of others are characterized by subordinate clauses. Some tend toward many layers of modification, some just a few here and there. Each choice has clear effects on rhythm and sound and sense.

Noun clusters, verb clusters, and absolutes are the most common.

IN THEIR NATURAL HABITAT

That's good thinking there, Cool Breeze. Cool Breeze is a kid with three or four days' beard sitting next to me on the stamped metal bottom of the open back of a pick up truck. Bouncing along. Dipping and rising and rolling on those rotten springs like a boat. Out the back of the truck the city of San Francisco is bouncing and streaming down the hill. One after another, electric signs with neon martini glasses lit up on them, the San Francisco symbol of "bar"—thousands of neon-magenta martini glasses bouncing and streaming down the hill, and beneath them hundreds, thousands of people wheeling around to look at this freaking crazed truck we're in, their white faces erupting from their lapels like marshmallows—streaming and bouncing down the hill—and God knows they have plenty to look at.

—*the opening paragraph of Tom Wolfe's* The Electric Kool-Aid Acid Test

"And nice to have seen you, Sue. Good luck," he called after her as she disappeared down the path, a pretty girl in a hurry, her smooth hair swinging, shining—just such a young woman as Nancy might have been. Then, starting home, he walked toward the trees, and under them, leaving behind him the big sky, the whisper of wind voices in the wind-bent wheat.

—the concluding paragraph of Truman Capote's In Cold Blood

Cumulatives occur in the midst of other constructions. Writers mix them up with short sentences and coordinate them in compound sentences and interrupt them with dashes and explanations. "And beneath them," for example, begins another independent clause within that sentence in Wolfe, launching another cumulative sentence. Wolfe breaks other pieces of cumulatives into deliberate fragments: "Bouncing along." Cumulatives sometimes begin with phrases, too, as in Capote's "Then, starting home."

What's most striking here is how the cumulative construction allows Wolfe and Capote to create very different effects. The Wolfe passage is frenetic and all in motion, a little "freaking" and "crazed" itself, the verb clusters and absolutes—and the very extension of the sentence, its continued unfolding—creating a sense of quick, blurry movement. The Capote passage is quiet. It's characterized by noun clusters and fixed, spatial images: the trees, the sky. The cumulative modifiers are shorter for him, drawing less attention to themselves, allowing the alliteration in the final line—all the *w* sounds—to create the final echoes.

USING ALL THIS FOR REVISION

*O*nce you have this key technology in mind—both nominalization and the cumulative—you can start revising your own freewriting and drafts, bringing out and coordinating what's implicit, recognizing and keeping what's already there. You don't ever need to write cumulatives as long and complicated as some of these. Knowing how just makes it easier for you to adapt the strategies to the quieter demands of your own writing.

Original:

It had been there three months since I traveled the road to the basketball coliseum on the nearby campus to start taking classes again. I actually reeled with shock when I saw the new paint job on the two sides of the coliseum. Now the newly painted sides vibrated with color. Three bright colors emphasized the protrusions at the roof line. I hadn't even noticed these protrusions before. Charcoal and dark neutrals set off the bright colors and outlined the structural parts of the building; sand color enlivened the major faces. The ramps and entryways on the lower half of the building had darker values of the brights and neutrals above to ground the building it seemed, and let the top soar. I couldn't stop looking at the building.

It was finally finished last week. The shades of very pleasant orange and red are punctuated at the top by strips of bright teal, an incongruous color since the school colors are orange and black. The contrasts work. The bright colors even soften and glow in the sunset. In our rain and fog they stand out as bright beacons, reminding us of the sun.

Revised:

It had been three months since I started traveling the road past the basketball coliseum, and I was reeling with shock. They were painting it! Suddenly the building vibrated with color, bright oranges emphasizing the protrusions of the roof life, a pale sand enlivening the major faces, charcoal and dark neutrals setting off the brightness, outlining the structure of the roof line and the buttresses. The ramps and entryways on the lower half had darker values of the brights and neutrals above, to ground the building, it seemed, let the top soar. I couldn't stop looking.

It was finally finished last week. The shades of pleasant orange and red are now punctuated at the top by strips of bright teal, an odd contrast, since the school colors are orange and black. But the contrasts work, the bright colors softening and glowing in the sunset, standing out like beacons in our rain and fog, reminding us of the sun.

You can see that what the writer has done is take complete sentences in the original and condense them into modifying phrases—mostly absolutes—to create a more flowing rhythm:

Suddenly the building vibrated with color,

bright oranges emphasizing the protrusions of the roof line, (ABS)

a pale sand enlivening the major faces,   (ABS)

charcoal and dark neutrals setting off the brightness,   (ABS)

outlining the structure of the roof line and the buttresses. (VC)

The revision is just as direct as the original. Nothing has been sacrificed that way. If anything, the revision is clearer since now the various details of the initial description are arranged in subordinate patterns, secondary details underneath major colors and impressions. The original seems scattered.

More is at stake here than simply cranking out cumulatives. It's a question of ear. Short sentences need to follow some of the longer ones, for example. That's the simplest dimension of sentence variety, but also finally the most important. The flowing cumulatives earn and prepare for the emphasis of short and direct sentences: "I couldn't stop looking."

Another example:

I always ride at least one ferry whenever I go to visit my brother. There is something wonderful about the half hour or so trip from Bremerton to Seattle. The boat wanders. It stops at places. People come and go, and I watch them. I seldom wonder where they come from or where they go when they get off. It doesn't matter. I'm sure they must have some place in mind. What does matter is the meandering trip, the stop and go, the cold wind on the observation desk, the chugging vibration of the engines that churn the water to green and white foam. And here is the rub.

Stephen always knows where he is going and what he will do when he arrives. In his efficient way Steve enjoys life. He plans and he strives. He makes decisions that are characteristically good. Perhaps that is why he heads the building committee at his church. They call to ask his advice and he freely gives it. It's a good position for an engineer. I have great respect for my brother. He knows a lot.

A few years ago I decided to go back to school. No one was more enthusiastic about it than Steve. At the time, I hadn't decided on a major. In fact, I hadn't really decided on anything, except that I wanted to find things out.

So, at the suggestion of my older brother, I returned to college as an engineering student. Steve had told me that the future was bright for engineers. He was right, of course. I attacked that future with zeal. I took all the math and science I could handle preparing myself for the really hard stuff that would come later.

I've taken several runs at calculus. Eventually I completed two of the four terms required for engineers. However, as things progressed, I began to founder. One day as my instructor droned more blue waves of confusion, I was too tired to fight any longer. It was like hitting an ephemeral wall. Halfway through class I turned to the fellow next to me and said, "Who gives a damn?" It felt so good to walk out of that class and close the door behind me. So ended my engineering aspirations. . . .

The strength of this original is the wonderful directness and unaffectedness of the sentences. "The boat wanders. It stops at places. People come and go, and I watch them." This sequence of four clauses has a gentleness and straightforwardness about it appropriate to the moment. It would be a shame to ruin that with mechanical combining. And yet as you read to the end of the passage, the shortness of the sentences starts to be too much. It starts sounding monotonous. When everything is emphasized through direct statement, it's hard to keep track of what's really central.

In the first paragraph the long sentence "What does matter is the meandering trip," for example, sets off the "boat wanders" sequence. It works. But later there isn't that kind of variety, and the piece starts to drag: "Steve had told me that the future was bright for engineers. He was right, of course. I attacked that future with zeal."

Not much tinkering is necessary to bring the rest to life, just a few adjustments here and there, not all of them cumulative structures but all in keeping with the logic of condensing and subordinating:

I always ride at least one ferry whenever I go to visit my brother. There is something wonderful about the half hour or so trip from Bremerton to Seattle. The boat wanders. It stops at places. People come and go, and I watch them. I seldom wonder where they come from or where they go when they get off. It doesn't matter. I'm sure they must have some place in mind. What does matter is the meandering trip, the stop and the go, the cold wind on the observation deck, the chugging vibration of the engines that churn the water to green and white foam. And here is the rub.

Stephen always knows where he is going and what he will do when he arrives. In his efficient way Steve enjoys life, planning and striving, making decisions that are characteristically good—which is maybe why he heads the building committee at his church. They call to ask his advice and he freely gives it, a good position for an engineer. I have great respect for my brother. He knows a lot.

A few years ago when I decided to go back to school, no one was more enthusiastic than Steve. At the time, I hadn't decided on a major—or on anything, except that I wanted to find things out.

At the suggestion of my older brother, I returned to college as an engineering student. Steve had told me that the future was bright for engineers, and he was right, of course. I attacked that future with zeal, taking all the math and science I could handle, preparing myself for the really hard stuff that could come later.

I've taken several runs at calculus, completing two of the four terms required for engineers, but as things progressed, I began to founder. One day as my instructor droned more blue waves of confusion, I was too tired to fight any longer. It was like hitting an ephemeral wall. Halfway through class I turned to the fellow next to me and said, "Who gives a damn?" It felt so good to walk out of that class and close the door behind me. So ended my engineering aspirations. . . .

Trailing modifiers liberate the short, unnominalized sentences, make them possible and resonant. And the patterns revealed then are in a sense "natural," already implicit in the freewritten draft. It's natural when composing quickly and without worrying about audience to fall into a rhythm of short and direct statement, simply describing what you see instead of trying to sound sophisticated. That's the key to a powerful style. What the cumulative technology allows you to do is capture that rhythm of direct saying without letting the directness turn into choppiness.

Freewriting makes available many sentences that can be condensed into cumulatives. It creates opportunities for combining.

There are lots of options here. There are various ways to revise. You could even argue that the originals in both cases are better. My point is simply to suggest how those options work and what notions of rhythm might guide them.

ACADEMIC WRITING

I've been insisting that these two strategies—trailing modifiers and avoiding nominalization—apply just as much to academic writing as to narrative writing, even though it's sometimes easier to illustrate them in narrations. Here are two examples.

A summary of an academic article (David Bartholomae's "Inventing the University") from a theory of rhetoric class:

> Even if students enter university as educated and literate individuals, they are still unfamiliar with the conventions of academic discourse. They are still outside the peculiar boundaries of the academic community and have to write their way into it. Most are aware that a special language is required for an academic classroom, but often they cannot control it. They have to speak the code of the powerful and wise before they know what they are doing. Their initial problem is to establish authority, to define rhetorically a position from which they may speak.
>
> Students have to learn to extend themselves by successive approximations into the commonplaces, set phrases, obligatory conclusions, and necessary connections that determine "what might be said" and which constitute knowledge within the various branches of the academic community. The movement towards a specialized discourse begins when a student can define a position of privilege that sets him against a "common" discourse, and when he can work self-consciously against not only the "common" code, but also his own, finding a compromise between personal history and the history of the discipline. The ability to imagine privilege enables writing.
>
> All writers must imagine for themselves the privilege of being insiders, that is, the privilege both of being inside an established and powerful discourse and of being granted a special right to speak. But that right to speak is seldom conferred on a writer because she has discovered an original idea. The moment of "eureka" is not simply a moment of breaking through a cognitive jumble in an individual writer's mind, but a moment of breaking into a familiar and established territory, one with insiders and outsiders, one with set phrases, examples, and conclusions.

What makes this summary work is the writer's decision to use concrete subjects and concrete verbs: students enter, they are still, they have to speak, students have to learn, all writers. It's this pattern of subject-verb declaration that gives the passage coherence, in fact, the repetition of "student" or "they" carrying the sequence of meaning all the way to the end, supplying a frame on which to hang these difficult abstractions. There are three key nominalizations as subjects: the movement, the ability, and the moment. But they work here. They work because the rest of the sentences are not nominalized. And they work because they are direct and straightforward themselves—not to mention evenly spaced in the passage, at parallel intervals. Finally there are the few trailing modifiers, not many of them, but enough to add texture and refine the major declarations of ideas: "to define rhetorically," "finding a compromise," "one with insiders."

Here is an explanation of a classic problem in elementary physics. The student had fifteen minutes to freewrite a response to the problem, then fifteen minutes to revise using COAP.

Suppose you put a big block of ice in a bucket and then fill the bucket with water until the water level is exactly even with the edge of the bucket. (The ice, of course, is now floating in the water.) Now wait for several hours for the ice to melt. Which of the following will happen? (Neglect evaporation.)

1.   The water level in the bucket will remain exactly the same.
2.   The water level in the bucket will drop.
3.   Some water will overflow the sides.

Imagine a clear glass beaker, filled with water to the level marked 1000 ml, kept in a room with 100 percent humidity to avoid evaporative losses. If you scoop out 100 ml and freeze it, you know what will happen: the water will slowly crystallize, expanding structurally, increasing in volume, but not in mass, giving water the somewhat rare property of being denser in its liquid than in its solid state.

Now when you return your frozen sample to the original beaker, think about what it is you are putting back in. You took away 100 ml, and froze it. You didn't add to it or subtract from it in mass or weight—you only changed its volume, a fraction of its total density. So when you slide the ice out of the small beaker, back into the large one, and the ripples have subsided, where will the water level settle? One thousand grams of water is still 1000 ml. The water level returns to the original water mark, two forms of the same substance each pooling their respective share of atoms, masses, volumes. The volume of ice flotating above the surface is merely that fraction corresponding to the decreased density.

And what are the alternatives? If you were to hold the ice down, the water level would certainly rise, temporarily, displacing its liquid self with the bulkier, solid state. But if you wait, the water mark would recede again, gradually, as the ice melts, finally reaching the starting point, achieving the density of the liquid state, volume reduced.

Usually solids of a given compound are denser than their liquid form; a solid will usually sink in a pool of its own liquid. If ice did not float, if it sank instead, the same experiment would show the level continually rising until all the ice had melted.[1]

There are at least two possible audiences for scientific writing: other scientists and the public. The syntax should be the same for both audiences, though the complexity of terminology might differ. There might be fewer metaphors when scientists talk with each other, certainly fewer analogies, examples, and definitions, since scientists don't need their common, shared understandings re-explained or taught. It's teaching that demands the simplest, most direct, most analogical approach.

This writer's response is by no means elementary or talking down. There are few analogies. What I admire about it is its use of the cumulative form and its concreteness and directness in the main clauses of those cumulatives:

The water level returns to the original water mark,

> two forms of the same substance each pooling their respective share of atoms, masses, volumes.   (*A*)

The cumulative allows the writer to make the general statement and then, cleanly and quickly, explain its subordinate parts. There don't need to be many cumulatives. The sentences don't need to be long. What makes them effective is the way that syntax reveals logical relationships:

---

[1]Adapted from John Bean, Dean Drenk, and F. D. Lee, "Microtheme Strategies for Developing Cognitive Skills," in C. W. Griffin, ed., *New Directions for Teaching and Learning: Teaching Writing in All Disciplines.*

The water will slowly crystallize,

expanding structurally,   (VC)

increasing in volume, but not in mass,   (VC)

giving water the somewhat rare property of being denser in its liquid than its solid state.   (VC)

There's also an effective variety of sentences, from short to long; effective use of punctuation—a dash especially; strong verb forms in "pooling," "scoop out," "slide." The imperative tense, the invitation to "imagine," mentally performing the actions being described, also gives the writing a directness and strength.

A number of earlier examples depend on the cumulative form: the summary of Thoreau's views on style (Chapter 2), the memo (Chapter 3), "Profit for Whom?" the structural imitation of Thomas (Chapter 4).

In a way it's really no big deal, and it's important to say that. Applying the free/style doesn't mean throwing caution to the winds, standing up on the lab table and breaking out into song. We're talking about syntax and diction here—technical strategies that can be used to convey any content, in any tone necessary. It's just a clearer prose this way.

SKETCHBOOK

✐ Write down all the nominalized sentences that cross your desk in a week and then rewrite them to make them more direct.

Write down all the cumulatives you find in your reading. Go look for them: in current issues of magazines, in any paperback book. Diagram and label.

And imitate these sentences, putting your content inside their structures. For example, here's a particularly long and lovely cumulative, a description of the earth, from Thomas's "The Corner of the Eye":

We are only now beginning to appreciate how strange and splendid it is, how it catches the breath, the loveliest object afloat around the sun, enclosed in its own blue bubble of atmosphere, manufacturing and breathing its own oxygen, fixing its own nitrogen from the air into its own soil, generating its own weather at the surface of its rain forests, constructing its own carapace from living parts: chalk cliffs, coral reefs, old fossils from earlier forms of life now covered by layers of new life meshed together around the globe, Troy upon Troy.

A student imitation:

We are only now beginning to appreciate how complex and fragile the forest really is, how it resists simple models, one of the most delicate ecosystems on the planet, canopied by its vast roof of branches, manufacturing oxygen, fixing nitrogen into the soil, generating its own soil from decaying logs and leaves, providing food and shelter for a wealth of birds and small animals: red-tailed hawks, Oregon Junco, field mice and chipmunks and possums, species on species.

REVISION

✐ Revise the first or second practice piece in light of this discussion. Take out the nominalizations and rephrase directly. Create sentence variety by strategic blending, transforming some sentences into modifying phrases. Create texture by adding new phrases.

....

6

TRICKS OF THE TRADE

Grammar is a piano I play by ear, since I seem to have been out of school the year the rules were mentioned. All I know about grammar is its infinite power. To shift the structure of a sentence alters the meaning of that sentence, as definitely and inflexibly as the position of a camera alters the meaning of the object photographed. Many people know about camera angles now, but not so many know about sentences. The arrangement of words matters, and the arrangement you want can be found in the picture in your mind.

—Joan Didion, "Why I Write"

*T*his chapter is a grab bag—a miscellany of strategies and notions of style left over after nominalization and the cumulative. Some of these strategies are refinements of the cumulative structure, ways of intensifying it and giving it emphasis. Others go beyond the cumulative structure: they're structures of brevity or parallelism that rhythmically check the cumulative's ebb and flow.

Nominalization and the cumulative are not all there is, in short. There are these other kinds of sentences and phrases, equally important, that the cumulative sets up or makes possible. Without them the cumulative would have no power, and vice versa. It's a question of variety and contrast. It's a question of ear: mixing and varying these tricks of the trade to create a pleasing or emphatic rhythm, an appropriate rhythm.

Style happens in the tensions between long and short sentences, loose and periodic, smooth and abrupt. It happens between the lines.

MORE ON THE CUMULATIVE: PUNCTUATION AND POSITIONING

Phrases at the Beginning and in the Middle

Though published writers put modifying phrases at the end most of the time, it's also effective to put modifying phrases at the beginning or in the middle of sentences. There can be rhythmic advantages to setting the stage in advance or briefly interrupting the movement of the statement:

> Paralyzed by the neurotic lassitude engendered by meeting one's past at every turn, around every corner, inside every cupboard, I go aimlessly from room to room.

The suspension or postponement created by the opening adjective cluster—and the subsequent series of prepositional phrases—mirrors the lassitude Didion feels.

Within just a few feet from your face, on either side, beavers and otters
are at play . . .

Swept off my feet, I floated from one side to the other, swiveling my
brain, staring astounded at the beavers, then the otters.

The first sentence we saw before: the opening modification is stage
setting. The short adjective cluster at the beginning of the second sentence establishes the attitude or tone controlling the rest of the sentence.

Interrupting modification:
I say, in the oblique way my family talks, that I will come.

These brief interruptions add texture and detail just as trailing modifiers
do, but they modify along the way, before the main part of the sentence
is completed.

A Cumulative as Part of a Compound Sentence

A compound sentence contains at least two independent clauses—
complete sentences—hooked together with "and" or "or" or "but."

She is an open and trusting child, unprepared for and unaccustomed to
the ambushes of family life, and perhaps it is just as well that I can offer
her little of that life.

The first independent clause here is cumulative, the phrase starting with
"unprepared for" modifying the main sentence. Didion then adds an
"and" and begins a new clause, coordinate with rather than subordinate
to the cumulative, which remains unmodified itself.

Commas and the Cumulative

The cumulative gives us one window on the complicated question of
commas. Cumulative modifiers are almost always "nonrestrictive"
phrases or clauses—additions not logically or syntactically necessary to

the sentence. The sentence can stand alone without them. These phrases need commas.

Opening phrases need to be followed by a comma:

Swept off my feet, I floated . . .

Trailing modifiers need to be preceded by a comma:

Sometimes it seems we take a loss, working this way.

If there's a series of trailing modifiers, each one needs to be preceded by a comma (the phrases in the middle are then nested within commas):

. . . underwater and on the surface, swimming toward your face and then away, more filled with life than any creatures I have ever seen before, in all my days.

Interrupting phrases are bracketed with commas, as if in parentheses:

I say, in the oblique way my family talks, that I will come.

One key to punctuation, then, is imagining the main part of the sentence as a simple subject-verb-object declaration that has phrases added to it at the beginning, middle, or end. Additions need to be handled with some sort of punctuation.

Subordinate clauses or phrases can also be "restrictive," necessary for the meaning of the sentence and so not set off with commas:

He is the man who can do the job. [Not just any man but *the* man. The "who" clause is necessary for the meaning of the sentence.]

This is the situation that I was telling you about. [Not just any situation but this specific one. The "that" clause doesn't add refining detail but necessary pieces of the main statement. It's essential.]

Fragments and Comma Splices

Two frequent errors start showing up when writers begin experimenting with the cumulative.

A fragment is usually a trailing modifier that's been broken off and punctuated separately. The writer is uneasy about writing a sentence that's too long, senses the break between the end of the main clause and the beginning of the modifiers, and puts in a period. The result is an incomplete sentence punctuated as complete—confusing for readers. The solution is simply to change the period to a comma:

> My childhood home was equipped with a real library. A room filled with books of classic fiction, scientific studies, philosophy, pulp novels, biographies, poetry and geography. [A noun cluster is broken off. Just change the period to a comma.]

> I am the eldest daughter of overeducated parents. A twice-degreed politician-Father and thrice-degreed Shakespeare-quoting Mother. [Another noun cluster broken off.]

> Jeffrey never intended to get in hot water or veer from the straight and narrow. Almost accidentally stealing the Cadillac, unthinkingly. [A verb cluster that needs a preceding comma rather than a period.]

A comma splice is the opposite problem. Instead of punctuating a subordinate phrase as complete, you punctuate a complete sentence as subordinate. That is, a comma splice is two complete sentences hooked together with a comma:

> My mother is the only other writer in our house, she was the one who could help me with all my English homework and help my writing.

> Whether my writing is considered good or bad is in the eye of the reader, however, the enjoyment of writing is in my own ear.

In the first example the two sentences flow together, are more connected than usual, a pairing. I think that's why the writer didn't want a period. It would seem too harsh or sudden, interrupt the flow. But though the writer's instinct is understandable, her use of punctuation is still wrong. Complete sentences need to be separated with periods or semicolons, however they are related rhythmically. If that relationship exists anyway, the period won't violate it for the reader. Readers read faster than writers, aren't disturbed by terminal punctuation—only by the lack of it. In the second example the student has been thrown off by the word "however" (like the word "therefore" or "thus"), which is not a coordinating word like "and" or "or." There needs to be a period or a semicolon.

The Semicolon

The semicolon is misnamed. It's not a semi*colon* but a semi*period*. Most of the time, if you can't use a period, you can't use a semicolon. Its function is to connect complete sentences that are closely related conceptually and rhythmically as well as roughly equivalent in length.

> It put me in a position where I could rely on mere raw ability and even my reputation occasionally; never having to put forth any genuine effort.

This is a common error. Uncertain about the length of the sentence, the writer pauses at the break between the main clause and the trailing verb cluster, using the semicolon like a hard comma instead of a soft period. In effect, the problem here is just like the problem with a fragment— since the semicolon functions like a period—and the solution is the same: make the semicolon (semiperiod) into a comma.

> I sweated and worked for hours; I worked on that thing until I finally got it done.

This is correct. The semicolon draws the two sentences together in our minds while recognizing that they are grammatically independent.

Almost all punctuation boils down to these simple differences between what's complete and what isn't, what needs to be represented as independent and what needs to be coordinated. It's all a question of relationship and how to represent relationships graphically.

Dangling Modifiers

Another common problem, a problem of positioning, is the dangling modifier:

> Standing at the bottom of the hill, the trail shot up ahead of me.

It's not the trail that is standing at the bottom of the hill, of course, but the writer. It's "I." The sentence should read:

Standing at the bottom of the hill, I watched the trail shoot up ahead of me.

Phrases—these are usually verb phrases—preceding a main clause always modify the subject of the clause. Writers who lose sight of this are often uneasy about using "I" or some other concrete subject as the grammatical subject of the sentence. They're worried about sounding too direct or straightforward and so back into the sentence, hide their own involvement in it.

INTENSIFYING THE CUMULATIVE: ROUGHNESS AND REPETITION

Parallel Repetition

A simple, effective strategy is to rephrase the final word or phrase of a sentence in another, parallel word or phrase. If you've ended with an adjective, add another adjective; if you've ended with a noun or noun phrase, add another noun or noun phrase that repeats the same idea, emphasizes it. It doesn't matter what the element is; just repeat it.

Here are some sentences I've culled from a recent batch of student freewriting—good, workable sentences:

Water makes me feel free, exploratory.

I was hooked, obsessed.

I could feel it getting colder, more passively aggressive.

They want to be judged, to be interpreted.

They were something I could hold on to, something lasting.

I have always been an editor, a critic of my own writing. The result is rigidity, writing that is cold and stiff.

I need direction, ideas that lead somewhere.

I watch myself being obsessed, watch my slip in control.

Maybe I have never really been in love, never really given myself to an experience.

Something about the rhythm of it felt familiar, meshed with my longing for stability, permanence.

Open-ended writing will allow me to let it all hang out, explore myself, find out where I'm particularly frigid.

In the cumulatives I described in the last chapter you add modifying phrases of varying kinds to refine the initial statement—verb clusters, noun clusters, absolutes, and so on. Here you only add the same kind of phrase or word you ended with. The phrase is parallel, on the same level. The effect, then, is one of repetition rather than refinement. It's an effect of intensification.

It's as if you're thinking aloud for a split second, searching for a synonym, a better way of saying what you just said. There's an impression of spontaneity:

I have been finding this reading a distraction, as if I have to put aside what I am doing, what is obsessing me, what matters to me—as if all this has nothing to do with my life, as if I can separate their lives, their struggles, from my own.

Here there's not just one repeated phrase but a series of them, a chain of parallel rephrasings, the thinking and the writing apparently simultaneous. Rather than stopping to choose the one right word, the writer seems to be sharing her search for the right words, putting all the options in front of us, in a line.

These kinds of rephrasings are natural to freewriting, appear naturally, as we think in and through the writing. Keeping them for the finished product is one way of keeping the energy and movement of those beginning bursts of words.

There's often an abruptness, a roughness to them. There's just a comma and then the new version ("abruptness, roughness"), and so as readers we're tripped up for a split second. But not in a bad sense. Our attention falls on the new word. There's no intervening rhythm or beat to let us smooth over it but a gap, a jump, that makes us pay attention. The predictable rhythm has been violated. There's a little bump or jerk, a jab.

Two examples from Didion:

There was no particular sense of moment about this, none of the effect of romantic degradation, of dark journey, for which my generation strived so assiduously.

The phrase "none of the effect" is a different version of "no particular sense," another way of saying the same thing, part of which is itself then restated, emphasized, in "of dark journey."

> Sometimes I think that those of us who are now in our thirties were born into the last generation to carry the burden of "home," to find in family life the source of all tension and drama.

Here Didion repeats the verb phrase to create a longer, more balanced rhythm.

Some examples from other contemporary essayists:

> I might learn something of mindlessness, something of the purity of living in the physical senses and the dignity of living without bias or motive.

> I think it would be well, and proper, and obedient, and pure, to grasp your one necessity and not let it go, to dangle from it limp wherever it takes you.

> *—Annie Dillard*

> I was not prepared for the St. John River, did not anticipate its size.

> *—John McPhee*

The short McPhee sentence is a good example of the extra emphaticness of the repeated verb. Two predicates are put side by side without smoothing connections, the writer seeming to start over again in the middle.

Emphatic Noun Clusters

As I briefly noted in the last chapter, one particularly effective version of this strategy of repetition is the simple noun cluster emphasizing the initial statement:

> This chapter is a grab bag—a miscellany of strategies and notions of style left over after the nominalization and the cumulative.

Some of these strategies are refinements of the cumulative structure, ways of intensifying it and giving it emphasis.

There's nothing fancy about this. It's just a way of bringing the point home, making it clearer and stronger. Often the movement is from a general statement to a clarification of it in slightly more specific terms. Thomas and Didion:

> I came away from the zoo with something, a piece of news about myself.

> We get along very well, veterans of a guerrilla war we never understood.

And it comes easily to students:

> I need control—strict control.

> I need direction, ideas that lead somewhere.

Notice that the noun cluster can literally repeat the previous noun ("I need control—strict control") or be a rephrasing of that noun, another version of it in different words ("I came away from the zoo with something, a piece of news about myself.").

Emphatic Adjective Clusters

There's much the same effect with an adjective cluster added after a noun phrase. The adjective quickly describes the qualities implicit in the subject of the sentence or the noun of the noun phrase:

> There was an unfortunate tendency to cast the foresters and researchers as forest-raping bad guys, all malevolence and profit-motive.

> It has been vandalized since my last visit and the monuments are broken, overturned in the dry grass.

> *—Joan Didion*

> The bear turned away, bored.

> *—John McPhee*

Emphatic Series

Related to these strategies of repetition and emphasis is the use of parallel elements in a series—not synonyms so much as different pieces or dimensions of the image or concept, piled up all at once. This is one of Thomas's strategies in "The Tucson Zoo":

> They are crazy little instruments, inhuman, incapable of controlling themselves, lacking manners, lacking souls.

> It is a debasement, a loss of individuality, a violation of human nature, an unnatural act.

In both these sentences the impression is of Thomas searching for the right word, trying to hit on just the right detail or image to make his point. It's an effect that depends on the omission of the "or" or "and" that might more typically go between the penultimate and ultimate element in the series. An "and" would ruin the series, make it too smooth or loose. Leaving it out tightens up the rhythm.

Notice the interesting asymmetry possible in these series: not three elements in a row, somehow the expected rhythm always, but two, or four, or five.

The omission of connectives is also the principle of emphasis in these two lists of details:

> I know this is autumn—the end of seasons—but this is the beginning of a new year of programs for us, new classes, new workshops, new meetings, new friends.

> Once there I fall into their ways, which are difficult, oblique, deliberately inarticulate, not my husband's ways.

Successive Verbs

Still another variation: not two verbs in a row, the second repeating the first, but two or more different or successive verbs:

> I would have liked to tell them of the options, explain my notations.

There are two actions here, telling and explaining, related but not the same. John McPhee often uses this strategy of succession:

I scuff a boot, take a break for a shiver in the bones.

She stops, turns, glowers.

He picks his moment, leaps, arches his back (ball behind his head), scores.

Colons and Dashes

Sometimes it's effective to emphasize these trailing repetitions and elucidations with a colon. It's as if there's an equal sign then between the main clause and the rephrasing of it. The rephrasing explains what was inside the main clause, unpacks it, the colon implying a "what I mean is" or "for example":

As I now recall it, there was only one sensation in my head: pure elation mixed with amazement at such perfection.

I speak in the tour-talk mode: technically simplified but with the correct amount of jargon.

He wants us to write our own sentences: to write with the syntax that already exists within our mind.

Dashes serve the same purpose, though more informally or loosely. The dash is a more informal colon, not implying an exact equivalence. What follows has the quality of an afterthought—or a punch line:

I need control—strict control.

This chapter is a grab bag—a miscellany of strategies and notions of style left over after nominalization and the cumulative.

Related to these strategies of repetition and emphasis is the use of parallel elements in a series—not synonyms so much as different pieces or dimensions of the image or concept, piled up all at once.

I went on the tour—personally conducted myself.

The colon and the dash are ways of emphasizing with punctuation the relationship that's always there with repetitive constructions: a relationship of equivalence and addition—of parallel rephrasing. And it's a question of choice. With any given concluding phrase you can choose a colon or a dash as a connector or emphasizer, the colon indicating one kind of relationship, the dash another.

Dashes and colons can set off any concluding phrase, whether it's parallel or repetitive or a grammatically new addition: adding a verb phrase to a noun, for example, as I've just done here.

The colon and the dash are also options for fixing the fragments I listed earlier. Often students fall into fragments because they instinctively want to indicate the kinds of relationships, of breaks, that dashes and colons represent:

> My childhood was equipped with a real library—a room filled with books of classic fiction, scientific studies, philosophy, pulp novels, biographies, poetry and geography.

> Jeffrey never intended to get in hot water or veer off the straight and narrow—almost accidentally stealing the Cadillac, unthinkingly.

or

> My childhood home was equipped with a real library: a room filled with books of classic fiction, scientific studies, philosophy, pulp novels, biographies, poetry and geography.

> I am the eldest daughter of overeducated parents: a twice-degreed politician Father and thrice-degreed Shakespeare-quoting Mother.

A dash, incidentally, is two hyphens. Using just one hyphen to indicate a dash is confusing.

Finally, dashes are useful for indicating interjected material in the middle of sentences. Dashes on both sides of the phrase make it clear that it's been added in parenthetically, though the phrase appears less peripheral then than it does between parentheses. Dashes make the phrase seem immediate and relevant somehow; parentheses make it seem like an aside.

Fragments

Now and then fragments can be effective. They can be deliberate, the period and the brief blank space at the end of the main sentence serving the same function as a colon or dash, only more emphatically, more visually. More obviously.

That last fragment seems deliberate—not just because it's about fragments—but because it's a parallel rephrasing of "more emphatically" and "more visually." It's broken off the series.

Fragments are also useful as quick lead-ins, functioning as titles or subheadings:

Now the second part of the secret.

Professional, published writers put their modifiers at the end of the sentences two thirds of the time . . .

Interrupting Repetitions

Of course, writers can also use repetition and rephrasing—just as they can with any sort of cumulative modifier—in the middle of sentences or phrases:

He seems to understand—to know, to see—me before I do.

The kind of car I want, the only car worth buying now, is the kind my brother has.

The older fellow next to him, the one in the nicest suit, the one without the name tag, asks him something and things get quieter. They step closer.

There's no intervening rhythm or beat to let us smooth over it but a gap, a jump, that makes us pay attention.

In all these cases the effect is of parentheses and addition. A new version or a clarification has occurred to the writer in the act of writing the first word or phrase and it's necessary, briefly, to insert that new thought. The insertion creates a momentary suspense, as well as another layer of meaning, another level of detail.

Asyndeton

The classical rhetoricians called the roughness or emphaticness I'm praising in some of these examples *asyndeton*. "I came, I saw, I conquered" is the most famous example of omitted connectives, as opposed to "Coming, I saw and then subsequently conquered"—a considerably less powerful version. In the same way, "Picking his moment, he leaps

and arches his back to score" is just not as interesting a sentence rhythmically as McPhee's original. A student example:

> Life is to be appreciated, cherished—not "spent."

> *versus*

> Life is to be appreciated and cherished rather than spent.

The abruptness of the original, its jamming together of elements, at-
tracts attention, is stronger on the page.

The effectiveness of much cumulative rephrasing also depends on
asyndeton. Part of the attraction of parallel repetition comes from the
little bump, the boost, that takes place between the comma and the
inserted or added phrase:

> I have always been an editor, a critic of my own writing. The result is
> rigidity, writing that is cold and stiff.

> *versus*

> I have always been an editor and critic of my own writing with the result
> that there's a rigidity in my words that makes my writing cold and stiff.

The original phrasings give the sentence a force and directness entirely
smoothed out in the revision, made limp. The revision *is* cold and rigid.
The original has a strength contradicting its claim.

There are degrees of roughness. Sometimes rephrasing creates a
smoother effect, depending on the weight and length of the main clause
and the trailing phrase or phrases.

Polysyndeton

Writers can also do the opposite, inserting conjunctions between every
element in a series, what classical rhetoric called *polysyndeton*. Not "I
came, I saw, I conquered" but "I came and I saw and I conquered."
There's a pleasing roughness or unpredictability about this, too, but it
comes more from a quality of running or hopping or loping. Like the
omission of connectives, the multiple conjunctions imply thinking
aloud. The writer isn't stopping to subordinate ideas in modifying
phrases but is just adding them on as she goes:

. . . the yellow fields and the cottonwoods and the rivers rising and falling and the mountain roads closing when the heavy snow comes in.

I would like to promise her that she will grow up with a sense of her cousins *and* of rivers *and* of her great-grandmother's teacups, would like to pledge her a picnic on a river with fried chicken *and* her hair uncombed . . .

In this second example the asyndeton is contained within phrases linked through polysyndeton. Similarly, in Dillard:

I think it would be well, and proper, and obedient, and pure, to grasp your one necessity and not let it go, to dangle from it limp wherever it takes you.

This is a strategy of emphasis, calling attention to words, violating a smooth or ordinary rhythm.

BEYOND THE CUMULATIVE: THE BEAUTY OF THE SHORT SENTENCE

The Single Short Sentence

Not every sentence you write should be heavily modified. Not every sentence should be long. One of the most effective strategies you can use as a writer, for example, is the short, emphatic sentence following longer sentences:

. . . within just a few feet from your face, on either side, beavers and otters are at play, underwater and on the surface, swimming toward your face and then away, more filled with life than any creatures I have ever seen before, in all my days. Except for the glass, you could reach across and touch them.
    I was transfixed. As I now recall it . . .

. . . I became a behavioral scientist, an experimental psychologist, an ethologist, and in the instant I lost all the wonder and the sense of being overwhelmed. I was flattened.

"I was transfixed" and "I was flattened" are the two sentences that most ring in my mind from "The Tucson Zoo," along with "Everyone says, stay away from ants." The principle is simply variety, a long, flowing sentence followed by a short one, emphatic in contrast. There's an element of surprise here.

Didion does much the same thing in her opening paragraph, writing the several long cumulative sentences ("We live in dusty houses," "Nor does he understand"), creating a long, flowing rhythm, then concluding the paragraph with a short, ringing phrase: "Marriage is the classic betrayal." It's a summarizing phrase, stating in general terms what the previous longer sentences have specified and given examples of, just as "I was transfixed" in the Thomas passage is a clincher, a concluding generalization for all that's come before.

The paragraph begins with a short, direct statement as well—"I am home for my daughter's first birthday"—which the subsequent sentences can be seen as elaborating and complicating before the concluding declaration.

Inexperienced writers rarely have the courage to write a short sentence on purpose. They don't want to appear unsophisticated. There's pressure on all of us to cover up and inflate and obscure. The wonderful brevity of these moments in Thomas and Didion teaches a different lesson entirely. Good writing depends not on obfuscation but on straightforward saying.

What gives short sentences their power is their rareness. We live in a world of palaver and bombast, of empty promises, everything inflated for salesmanship or status. People just don't expect writers to come out and say what they mean. When you do, you catch them by surprise, make them sit up and notice.

Pairs of Short Sentences

Pairs of short sentences play off each other. The second rephrases the first. (As I've just done here.) Or:

The stars are out! They are wheeling in the sky!

The cats are meowing. They want to eat.

The second sentence functions exactly like the parallel rephrasings of a cumulative sentence, only the new detail or clarification is stated as an

independent clause. The rhythm of it is different, too, deliberately chop-
pier, as opposed to "The stars are out, wheeling in the sky." The notion
of wheeling isn't featured or set off as strongly when it's subordinated.
Subordination deemphasizes. Declaration emphasizes:

> But I came away from the zoo with something, a piece of news about
> myself: I am coded, somehow, for otters and beavers.

A colon indicates the relationship between these two balanced declarations in Thomas. Colons, semicolons, and dashes can join complete
sentences a degree more in our minds, represent a closer relationship
than usually exists between sentences, functioning in that sense just this
side of subordination.

> Days pass. I see no one.

> Questions trail off, answers are abandoned, the baby plays with the dust
> motes in a shaft of afternoon sun.

The relationship among these sentences in Didion is one of succession
or sequence rather than equivalence or modification. These are separate
actions. Putting them together flatly and without connectives suggests
rhythmically the flatness of the experience for Didion, the emptiness.

Obviously asyndeton is one of the features of these pairings or
successions. Short sentences are still rougher—less smooth and
symmetrical—than the parallel rephrasings that I described in the last
section.

Series of Short Sentences

These effects can be extended over a longer series of direct sentences:

> I was transfixed. As I now recall it, there was only one sensation in my
> head: pure elation mixed with amazement at such perfection. Swept off
> my feet, I floated from one side to the other, swiveling my brain, staring
> astounded at the beavers, then at the otters. I could hear shouts across
> my corpus callosum, from one hemisphere to the other. I remember
> thinking, with what was left in charge of my consciousness, that I wanted
> no part of the science of beavers and otters; I wanted never to know how
> they performed their marvels; I wished for no news about the physiol-

ogy of their breathing, the coordination of their muscles, their vision, their endocrine systems, their digestive tracts. I hoped never to have to think of them as collections of cells. All I asked for was the full hairy complexity, then in front of my eyes, of whole, intact beavers and otters in motion.

This is a good example of all the strategies I've been talking about in this and the last chapter: trailing modifiers, opening and interrupting modifiers, elements in a series, omitted connectives. At their heart is the series of four "I" declarations: "I remember," "I wanted," "I wished," "I hoped." (Actually, every sentence in this paragraph is built around a declaration beginning with "I"; these are just the four without additional modification.) Rhetorically they serve the same purpose as free modifiers in a cumulative sentence, refining and expanding the initial statement, "I wanted no part of the science of beavers and otters." The semicolons indicate their parallel relationship. The effect finally is emphasis. The stress falls both on "I" and on Thomas's desire *not* to overanalyze his experience—that point repeated four times.

Another example from John McPhee, a description of a grizzly bear in Alaska:

He picked up the salmon, roughly ten pounds of fish, and, holding it with one paw, he began to whirl it around his head. Apparently, he was not hungry, and this was a form of play. He played sling-the-salmon. With his claws embedded near the tail, he whirled the salmon and then tossed it high, end over end. As it fell, he scooped it up and slung it around his head again, lariat salmon, and again he tossed it into the air. He caught it and heaved it once more. The fish flopped to the ground. The bear turned away, bored. He began to move upstream by the edge of the river. Behind his big head his hump projected. His brown fur rippled like a field under wind. He kept coming. The breeze was behind him. He had not yet seen us. He was romping along at an easy walk. The single Slepper, with John Kauffman in it, moved up against a snagged stick and broke it off. The snap was light, but enough to stop the bear. Instantly, he was motionless and alert, roaming on his four feet and straining his eyes to see. We drifted toward him. At least, we arrived in his focus. If we were looking at something we had rarely seen before, God help him so was he. If he was a tenth as awed as I was, he could not have moved a muscle, which he did now, in a hurry that was not pronounced but nonetheless seemed inappropriate to his status in the situation. He crossed low ground and went up a bank toward a copse of willow. He stopped there and faced us again. Then, breaking stems to pieces, he went into the willows.

In this passage, too, you can see all the devices of the cumulative used for variety and contrast. There are some trailing modifiers, some introductory modification. But the description depends on short, subject-verb sentences: "He had not yet seen us," "we drifted toward him." The reliance on brevity is so marked it soon becomes an obvious strategy, a lack of stylishness that becomes stylish. It's as if McPhee is whispering, so scared he's forgotten how to subordinate. The shortness of the sentences slows us down, forces us to attend to every detail as if it's separate from others, all of them of equal importance. Nothing is subordinated in the experience.

We could translate some of these short statements into cumulatives:

> The bear turned away, bored, moving upstream by the edge of the river, his hump projecting behind his big head, his brown fur rippling like a field under wind.

A good way to understand the syntax of modification is to imagine each modifier as originally or potentially a complete statement, a short subject-verb declaration. Your choice as a writer, then, is what to subordinate and what not to. Effects result from those choices. Here, although the cumulative sentence is fine, even good, it doesn't fit the circumstance. It's not as powerful as the deliberately brief and emphatic sentences McPhee has piled together. The roughness, the choppiness, works.

Notice how the sentence "If he was a tenth as awed as I was, he could not have moved . . ." stands out from the rest, almost officious and bureaucratic. In the context of the whole passage I can't help but see it as a parody of wordiness meant to highlight how "inappropriate" human verbiage is in the face of a grizzly.

Compound Sentences

The McPhee passage also highlights the value of coordination, of the compound sentence:

He picked up the salmon, roughly ten pounds of fish, and, holding it with one paw, he began to whirl it around his head. Apparently, he was not hungry, and this was a form of play. He played sling-the-salmon. With his claws embedded near the tail, he whirled the salmon and then tossed it high, end over end.

"Ands" and "buts" and "ors" simply allow you to put two or more complete sentences together, smoothing and blending slightly without losing directness. You can suggest degrees of balance and imbalance.

"And then tossed it high" is an example of a compound predicate, a new expression of the verb with the original subject implied ("he").

Beginning with *And* and *Or*

Sometimes its effective to begin sentences with "and" or "or" to suggest an apparently spontaneous addition. It's another variety of polysyndeton:

You can use the device to separate phrases within the sentence. Or you can use it across whole sentences, indicating skips and jumps of thought. Or you don't have to use it at all.

BALANCE AND PARALLELISM AND SMOOTHNESS

*I*t's obvious that all the strategies I've been talking about under the headings of cumulative structure or roughness and rephrasing lead to a certain range of styles. There *is* a range, a wide possibility of voices, from Capote to Wolfe, Dillard to McPhee, but these voices all have a syntax and a sense of stylistic options in common. They are all varieties of what I've called the free/ style. The tricks of the trade I've discussed here are tricks of the free/ style, some features of language to recognize in freewriting and keep, or to put into your writing through revision however it's produced.

But this is not the only style, and these are not the only compelling features of written language. Smoothness can be good, too. Balance and parallelism can also have power. The periodic sentence can have an expressiveness the cumulative lacks.

Proverbs, Quotes, and Jokes

Many proverbs are periodic sentences:

> It is better to have loved and lost than never to have loved at all.

> It is better to give than to receive.

As in all periodic sentences, these aren't over until they're over. The comparative at the beginning establishes a suspense that isn't over until the comparison is made. The comparison depends on a balance of elements: loved and lost / never to have loved; to give / to receive. It's this kind of balance and tension that makes a quotable quote quotable:

> Ask not what your country can do for you but what you can do for your country.

Classical rhetoricians would call this famous statement an example of *antimetabole*, the repetition of words in successive clauses in reverse grammatical order. There were dozens, even hundreds of special figures like this in classical rhetoric—anaphora, polyptoton, anadiplosis, epistrophe, and so on. The terms aren't important in themselves. What's important for us is that these figures were deliberately artificial and ceremonial, ways of calling attention to language, usually through schemes of balance and pithiness. Pithiness implies forethought and planning and careful crafting in a way that the cumulative doesn't. And that can be powerful, particularly on a ceremonial, formal occasion.

Balance of this sort can also be the key to a joke, as in this from Woody Allen:

> Not only is there no God, but try getting a plumber on the weekend.

The punch line is set up through the suspension created by "not only is there no God," a construction that demands completion. The joke happens in the completion. Both sides of the sentence, the clauses on either side of the "but," are roughly the same size and weight.

Premeditated Parallelism

There are also other kinds of parallelism than the kind I've talked about, parallelism that suggests not thinking aloud but careful orchestration of crafted, prearranged elements:

Reading maketh a full man; conference a ready man; and writing an exact man. And therefore, if a man write little, he had need have a great memory; if he confer little, he had need have a present wit; and if he read little, he had need have much cunning, to seem to know what he doth not.

　　　—Francis Bacon

... for the support of this declaration, with a firm reliance on the protection of Divine Providence, we mutually pledge to each other our Lives, our Fortunes, and our sacred Honor.

　　　—Declaration of Independence

Smooth Cumulatives

For that matter, I don't want to exaggerate the roughness of the cumulative or suggest that roughness is endemic to any particular kind of phrasing in that structure. Cumulatives, too, can create effects of balance and smoothness:

> Science gets most of its information by the process of reductionism, exploring the details, then the details of the details, until all the smallest bits of the structure, or the smallest parts of the mechanisms, are laid out for counting and scrutiny.

To my ear there's an orderliness to the arrangement of the phrases in this sentence that reflects the kind of orderly scientific analysis Thomas is talking about. Didion's long noun cluster on the cottonwoods and the fields, lengthened as it is by the polysyndeton, also has a smoothing, longer rhythm:

> He does understand that when we talk about sale-leasebacks and right-of-way condemnations we are talking in code about the things we like best, the yellow fields and the cottonwoods and the rivers rising and falling and the mountain roads closing when the heavy snow comes in.

Notice, too, how the noun cluster is balanced in length and weight with the main part of the sentence.

Contrast and Variety

It's all a question of degree, and of our impressions as readers. And it's a question of contrast and variety. After all, the last sentence of the Thomas paragraph beginning with "I was transfixed" is a periodic sentence:

All I asked for was the full hairy complexity, then in front of my eyes, of whole, intact beavers and otters in motion.

Coming at the end of a long paragraph of parallel declarations, and in the context of an essay where Thomas relies, as he always does, on the cumulative form, the periodic sentence stands out. It has an extra, summarizing force.

A LIFE OF THEIR OWN

Two final applications of all this, the first personal, the second technical, both from students.

Original:

I've been working myself into a frenzy, a common enough experience, resisting all my thoughts, refusing to sit down, putting pen to paper, hating the thought of writing. I've run through all my rituals. The TV became my bartender for over two hours, talking to me, offering suggestions for refreshments every 15 minutes, soothing my ragged edges. It turned off a half hour ago, and since then I've wandered, restless and relentless, around the house, stalking my next amusement. I felt gritty, so I took a shower. I felt hungry, so I raided the kitchen: orange juice and pudding and water and chocolate chips. Then I retreated, disgusted with my spoils. I was tired, but I couldn't shut off my mind. So I finally returned to my room. Tension, anticipation caused my brain to jerk its thoughts out sporadically, blinding me with flashes of blankness; my body twitched nervously from toes to hands. My skin itched. Words fought me at every turn. Turned first away from my brain, they struggled to come out anyway, irritating my skin, grabbing at my hands, seeking to possess anything I could. I hunted down my pen and paper, set up the environment, and sat down to wait. Then I began to write, almost simply, easily. I had captured and been captured.

Revision:
  I've been working myself into a frenzy, resisting my thoughts, refusing to sit down, putting pen to paper, hating the thought of writing. I've run through my rituals. The TV became my bartender for hours, talking to me, offering suggestions for refreshment every 15 minutes, soothing my edges. It turned off a half hour ago, and since then I've wandered, restless and relentless, around the house, stalking. I felt gritty, so I took a shower. I felt hungry, so I raided the kitchen: orange juice and pudding and water and chocolate chips. Then I retreated, disgusted. I was tired, but I couldn't shut off my mind. I returned to my room. My brain jerked out thoughts, blinding me with blankness; my body twitched from toes to hands. My skin itched. Words fought me. Turned first away from my brain, they struggled to come out anyway, irritating my skin, grabbing at my hands, seeking to possess. I hunted down my pen and paper, set up the environment, sat down to wait. Then I began to write, almost simply, easily. I had captured and been captured.

I've cut a number of phrases here that are clichéd, too familiar: "ragged edges," "spoils," "twitched nervously," "at every turn." Truncated like this, the remaining words have a slightly startling effect: "soothing my edges." I've cut "all" several times. I've taken an "and" out of the third-to-the-last sentence, again for asyndeton. I've cut several phrases that aren't redundant so much as unnecessary: "a common enough experience," "my next amusement." Although these provide some new information, they're stuffy, ineffectual phrases. We can live without them, and the remaining sentences are then less obstructed, their strength able to stand out more. Finally, I've cut deeply into the "tension, anticipation" sentence, changing the subject to avoid the nominalizations, making the phrasing twitchier and jerkier.

Original:
  Beer is a popular drink in the United States. The beer industry makes up a large percentage of all beverages available on the market. It's obvious from the wide selection in the stores that there is a lot of competition for the consumer's dollar. Hop and malt are major contributors to beer aroma. It would be useful in product development or reformulation work to know the relationship of these two attributes in commercial

American beers. After all, if the aroma of a certain ingredient influences the overall aroma of the beer; it's important to know what the relationship of that ingredient is to other ingredients and to the product itself. How does it affect the overall aroma of the product and how does it affect the style of the beer? It would be useful information to know how hop and malt aromas differ among beer styles.

Commercial beers have two ingredients in common—hops and malt. Descriptors used to describe hoppy aroma in beer include spicy/herbal, citrus/floral, grapefruit, and grassy. Lager beers typically have cabbagy and vegetable odors. Some other common aromas in beer are banana, green apple, fruity, estery, pineapple, caramel, and sweet.

Styles of beer include premium, regular, light, and dark. Premium beers are those beers that the manufacturer has determined to be excellent in quality. Dark beers use a roasted malt to give a caramel, coffee, or molasses aroma quality. Light beer has medium carbonation, a touch of maltiness, and fewer calories. Regular style beer, or traditional lagers, have light body, bright and golden color, with some malt in the nose, and a slight hop flavor.

In this study our objective was to assess the relationship between hop and malt aroma based on the evaluation of major American beer brands and styles by a trained descriptive panel.

A series of flat, monotonal statements, full of nominalizations. It's hard to tell what the main point is. There's nothing to hold onto—no smell, except when the writer (a researcher in a campus laboratory) starts listing the wonderful vocabulary of aroma near the end: spicy/herbal, citrus/floral, and so on.

The free/style can make this introduction work far better, both as a communication of ideas and as a slightly more interesting, slightly more stylish piece of writing:

Revision:

Beer is popular in the United States. There's more beer on store shelves than any other drink—and many competing labels.

How can a beer-maker capture more customers?

Aroma is one key, and hops and malt are two key ingredients in the aroma of beer. How are these two ingredients related to each other and how, exactly, do they contribute to aroma? How are they related to other ingredients in beer? How do they relate to each other in different styles of beer?

To answer these questions we asked a trained descriptive panel to evaluate hop and malt aromas in major American beer brands and styles.

To describe hoppy aromas researchers often use terms like spicy/ herbal, citrus/floral, grapefruit, grassy—or other words like banana, green apple, fruity, estery, pineapple, caramel, and sweet. Lager beers typically have cabbagy and vegetable odors.

To describe the aroma of malt, researchers use other distinctions: dark beers use a roasted malt to give a caramel, coffee, or molasses quality to the aroma; light beer has medium carbonation, a touch of maltiness, and fewer calories; traditional lagers have light body, bright and gold color, some malt in the nose, and a slight hop flavor. . . .

First, the revision relies on concrete subjects and concrete verbs: "we asked," "researchers often use." Second, it uses the most concrete and homey nouns and verbs that it can: "beer-maker" instead of "manufacturer." In the opening sentences there's an effort to conjure up a faint image of a store shelf and of actual labels on beer bottles, although generally the revision keeps to the scientific, white-coated diction apparently necessary here: "evaluate," "ingredients." There's a nice balance. Colons and parallel constructions indicate the subordinate and coordinate relationships. (The semicolon mistake of the original has been corrected, too.)

There are two one-sentence paragraphs, for emphasis. In this version we know much sooner what the point of the study is (that's involved some moving of sentences, too). The blank space—a faint version of a collage (see the next chapter)—indicates the move from the introduction to the body of the report.

Style happens when words reach some sort of critical mass in excess of what's been put into them. Style happens when words take on a life of their own, and that depends on what you're writing about, on your audience, on luck, and on the words themselves. Sometimes it's as if the words are writing you, establishing their own rhythms, a main clause demanding a noun cluster, a noun cluster leading then to an absolute, and then the short sentence and colon necessary: right there. Or it comes through revision after revision and you have no idea what the words sound like anymore—you're frustrated and sick of it—and then looking at the page the next day, all those lines and arrows and crossed-out words everywhere, you realize that suddenly the passage makes sense and sounds good.

SKETCHBOOK

✐ Write down and imitate any sentences from your reading that strike you as strong, evocative, interesting.

REVISION

✐ Revise the first or second practice piece in light of this chapter.

7

PUSHING THE OUTSIDE OF THE ENVELOPE

I fear chiefly lest my expression may not be extra vagrant enough, may not wander far enough beyond the narrow limits of my daily experience so as to be adequate to the truth of which I have been convinced. . . . for I am convinced that I cannot exaggerate enough even to lay the foundation of a true expression.

—Thoreau, *Walden*

The standard non-fiction writer's voice was like the standard announcer's voice . . . a drag, a droning. . . . To avoid this I would try anything . . . it was a matter of personality, energy, drive, bravura . . . style in a word.

—Tom Wolfe, "The New Journalism"

*T*his chapter is on free/style deluxe —fancier and more daring turns on the same principles—the basic impulses unleashed and unabashed.

STRATEGY ONE: THE DRAMATIZATION OF THOUGHT

*T*he dramatization of thought is always implicit in freewriting and to some small degree always underneath the free/style, but this takes the dramatization further, makes it evident, exaggerates it.

Rather than working out a complicated problem in advance and then presenting a final thesis in the beginning, pat and finished, you simply present all the approaches and your thinking about each without taking sides, implying that all of them have some value. You think aloud on the page, in the now of the writing, or share the story of some past thinking, in chronological order. The organization is then both intellectual and narrative, a sequence of ideas as they occur. The dramatization of thought is a liberating strategy, making a virtue of complexity and containing it all in the larger, simple design of the process of trying to figure out that complexity. It makes it possible to include all the layers and shadings and so might be more accurate. It's also attention grabbing, a way of drawing readers into ideas, making ideas seem alive and real, concrete.

This isn't just freewriting: it's making the writing look like freewriting, but with more control and precision. The product has the structure of the process.

The TRIACing organization of "The Tucson Zoo" is contained in the larger structure of a story of Thomas's thinking. He begins with the experience with the beaver and otters and then tells the story of his thinking about that experience, its ups and downs, ebbs and flows, from "I was transfixed" to "I was flattened." The thinking and feeling are presented chronologically—"It lasted, I regret to say, for only a few minutes"—leading then to questions and thinking aloud in the now of this essay. "What was released? Behavior. What behavior? Standing, swiveling flabbergasted, feeling exultation and the rush of friendship." Questions, rather than answers, and the questions in their apparently natural order.

In "Late Night Thoughts on Mahler's Ninth Symphony," Thomas shares the ebbing and flowing of his moods as he listens to Mahler and explains how his responses have changed over time. "There was a time" when the music inspired in him "quiet celebration" and "tranquility." "Now I hear it differently," he says, as a suggestion of "death everywhere," "sadness," and then he goes on to a meditation on world events, the music swelling in the background. It's intimate, personal, apparently improvisational. We seem to be "overhearing" rather than "hearing" him.

The same structure organizes a paragraph from "Lives of a Cell":

> I have been trying to think of the earth as a kind of organism, but it is no go. I cannot think of it that way. It is too big, too complex, with too many working parts lacking visible connections. The other night, driving through a hilly, wooded part of New England, I wondered about this. If not like an organism, what is it like, what is it *most* like? Then, satisfactorily for that moment, it came to me: it is *most* like a single cell.

A story of thinking. Rather than illustrating a thesis statement, Thomas structures the paragraph around *finding* one, beginning with one possibility, rejecting it, then narrating the discovery of what—for a moment, at least—seems satisfactory.

There's a structure here to be imitated, within or across paragraphs. First describe a scene or incident or experience in your life and then go on to reflect on its meaning, unpack its significance. The structure of the essay is the structure of that unpacking. Write a "Late Night Thoughts on _____," sharing the ebbing and flowing. Put on music and record what happens inside you as you listen to it, "Late Night Thoughts on Listening to Paul Simon" or "Willie Nelson" or "Van Halen." Write a paragraph narrating the discovery of a possible thesis, describing where that discovery took place (in your car, on a walk, in the shower, at a party).

Didion, too, often dramatizes the process of her thinking, recreating the scene and circumstances of a specific struggle to understand, sharing the whole process of that struggle:

> As it happens I am in Death Valley, in a room at the Enterprise Motel and Trailer Park, and it is July, and it is hot. In fact it is 119. I cannot seem to make the air conditioner work, but there is a small refrigerator,

and I can wrap ice cubes in a towel and hold them against the small of my back. With the help of the ice cubes I have been trying to think, because The American Scholar asked me to, in some abstract way about "morality," a word I distrust more every day, but my mind veers inflexibly toward the particular.

Didion writes in the present tense, the thinking and the writing (apparently) simultaneous, happening before our eyes. It's located thinking, situated in a place and time. As the essay goes on, Didion tries out different answers to the question she has to address, considering the possibilities of each without rejecting any. "What does it mean?" she asks. "It means nothing manageable." She doesn't have the answers and so can only dramatize her own effort to find answers. At times the essay is like a conversation, Didion gesturing toward us, as if we're there, in the insufferably hot motel: "You are quite possibly impatient with me by now" but "let me tell you. . . ." There isn't a thesis at the beginning, figured out and then enforced in the rest of the essay. The movement is the movement of the mind, the ideas unfolding, shifting, changing.

There are elements of this strategy in "On Going Home": present tense narration ("I *am* home"), shifts of thought and thinking ("Or perhaps it is not anymore"), questioning ("Who is beside the point?"). And these suggest more strategies to imitate. Recreate the scene of your writing. Write in the present tense yourself. Ask questions.

Strategies of spontaneity are part of the tradition of the "essay"— the essay now as opposed to the more staid and conservative "article," not fixed and mechanical (what we normally mean by the word "essay" now), but open-ended, personal, exploratory. Essay in its original sense, a real *essayez*, or trying. Here's Montaigne, the father of the essay form, describing his method and the method of all subsequent essayists:

> I let my thoughts run on, weak and lowly as they are, as I have produced them, without plastering and sewing up the flaws.

> I take the first subject that chance offers. They are all equally good to me. And I never plan to develop them completely.

He writes, he says, "without a plan and without a promise," "without definitions, without divisions, without conclusions," "without any system." "My style and mind alike go roaming," and the result is a freer, more sophisticated form for representing thought:

I want the matter to make its own divisions. It shows well enough where it changes, where it concludes, where it begins, where it resumes, without my interlacing it with words, with links and seams introduced for the benefit of weak or heedless ears, and without writing glosses on myself.

The scholars distinguish and mark off their ideas more specifically and in detail. I, who cannot see beyond what I have learned from experience, without any system, present my ideas in a general way, and tentatively. As in this: I speak my meaning in disjointed parts, as something that cannot be said all at once and in a lump. Relatedness and conformity are not found in low and common minds such as ours.

When most of us hear the word "essay," as in "essay test" or a 1,000-word "essay" on beauty pageants or college sports or whatever, we think of just the opposite. Not open-endedness but closedness; not flexibility but rigidity. Yet the tradition of the essay, the tradition that Thomas and Didion are writing in, too, is a tradition of dramatizing intellectual process in a world where definitive answers aren't possible.

It's not that anything goes, no revision necessary. Montaigne "goes out of [his] way," but "rather by license than carelessness." The three volumes of his essays were revised and revised over years, new phrasing added, old phrases taken out. The appearance of spontaneity is deliberately calculated, not an easy thing to achieve. The goal is not to abandon structure but to find a subtler, more natural structure—as controlled as formulaic writing but controlled in a different way. The goal is to think more subtly, make the connections more sophisticated, truer to the complexities of the mind.

At the end of an essay on the "New Journalism," Tom Wolfe suddenly takes back his whole thesis, changing his mind (apparently) at the moment he's writing:

The status of the New Journalism is not secured by any means. In some quarters the contempt for it is boundless . . . even breathtaking. . . . With any luck at all the new genre will never be sanctified, never be exalted, never given a theology. I probably shouldn't even go around talking it up the way I have in this piece. All I meant to say when I started out was that the New Journalism can no longer be ignored in an artistic sense. The rest I take back. . . . The hell with it. . . . Let Chaos reign . . . louder music, more wine. . . .

The "New Journalism" is also part of this old tradition of making language come alive, reflect the natural cadences of thought. The story for Wolfe is that as a young reporter, overwhelmed by the complexity and intensity of the material he'd gathered for a story, days past deadline, he sat down, turned up the music, and let fly, writing a "memo" to his editor in a manic, all-at-once style, letting everything out, putting it all down without too much concern for the niceties. The result was "The Kandy-Kolored Tangerine-Flaked Streamline Baby" and the beginning of Wolfe's career as one of our preeminent prose stylists.

His goal, he says, is "to give the illusion not only of a person talking but of a person thinking." Ellipses, for example, suggest the pause as he stops to think of the next phrase, his motor still running. Sudden interjections reflect spontaneous reactions to his own material in his rush to go on to the next detail. On every level Wolfe wants his writing to appear "buoyant, free and easy, spontaneous."

The paradox is that "creating the effect of spontaneity in writing is one of the most difficult things you can do." Wolfe outlines, revises every day, sticks to a schedule, researches exhaustively.

Try creating buoyancy in your own writing. Turn up the music and let fly, then spend days revising—revising to reveal the subtleties of what was already there. Then take back the thesis in the final paragraph. Explain why.

STRATEGY TWO: AMPLIFICATION AND INTENSIFYING

A second strategy, related to the first, an extension of it, is pulling out all the rhetorical stops within a sentence, amplifying and lengthening it with device after device.

In the essay on the New Journalism Wolfe says that he'll "do anything" to grab the attention of the reader. The "pale beige" tone of conventional journalism seems "boring" and "pallid" to him and he'll do all he can to juice it up, energize it:

> In the training film the flight deck was a grand piece of gray geometry, perilous, to be sure, but an amazing abstract shape as one looks down upon it on the screen. And yet once the newcomer's two feet were on it . . . *Geometry*—my God, man, this is a . . . skillet! It *heaved*, it

moved up and down underneath his feet, it pitched up, it pitched down, it rolled to port (this great beast *rolled*!) and it rolled to starboard, as the ship moved into the wind and, therefore, into the waves, and the wind kept sweeping across, sixty feet up in the air out in the open sea, and there were no railings whatsoever. This was a *skillet*!—a frying pan!—a short-order grill!—not gray but black, smeared with skid marks from one end to the other and glistening with pools of hydraulic fluid and the occasional jet-fuel slick, all of it still hot, sticky, greasy, runny, virulent from God knows what traumas—still ablaze!—consumed in detonations, explosions, flames, combustion, roars, shrieks, whines, blasts, horrible shudders, fracturing impacts, as little men in screaming red and yellow and purple and green shirts with black Mickey Mouse helmets over their ears skittered about on the surface as if their very lives (you've said it now!), hooking fighter planes onto the catapult shuttles so that they can explode their afterburners and be slung off the deck in a red-mad fury with a *kaboom*! that pounds through the entire deck.

It's as if Wolfe is trying to push all the rhetorical buttons all at once, turn on the machine full blast, show off everything within the periods. It's as if he's taken the devices of the free/style and gone wild with them. Some of his strategies:

exclamations:	Skillet! Ablaze!
interjections:	this great beast rolled!
italics:	*rolled, skillet*
ellipsis:	my God, man, this is a . . . *skillet*!
parentheses:	(you've said it now!)
present tense narration:	this *is* a skillet
cumulative structure—lengthened, intensified:	the whole third sentence beginning with "It heaved . . ."
piling up of detail:	detonations, explosions, flames
metaphor:	skillet, frying pan, short-order grill

One of the paradoxes of the passage is that Wolfe pulls out these stops in an effort to represent the experience more fully. He wants the language to evoke the experience, correspond to it, help us have the experience of landing on an aircraft carrier *in* the experience of reading these words. And yet at the same time the language, in its density and interest, calls attention to itself. It doesn't just reflect the landing on the aircraft carrier but in a sense competes with it.

On the one hand, in other words, this is apparently spontaneous writing, a burst of words in the heat and enthusiasm of the moment—natural. And yet it's in this burst of words, in this enthusiasm, that Wolfe draws on all the devices of prose style he can find, turns on all the figures of the figurative tradition, all the punctuation of the New Journalism—becomes unnatural.

Wolfe is trying to show that he, too, has the right stuff of the fighter jocks, except in language. He's trying to push the outside of the envelope of words.

Two imitations, by teachers about teaching, freewrites then revised, all-out uses of words:

> Death holds no sway over the middle school teacher. Lock yourself into a pale-bleakgreen room the size of a large broom closet, without even an escape window, with 30 or so mewling, pimplefaced, hormone-infested thirteen-year-olds day in and day out for nine unremitting months out of the year, hear ten thousand times the odious teenage mantra: this is BOOORING and THEN see how you feel about death. See how you feel about death in mid-August, when you have only two more weeks (fourteen days times twenty-four, no, take ten hours off for nightmare therapy, fourteen times fourteen, that's onehundredninetysix short hours until SCHOOLSTARTS) of wide-open quietmorning sneerfree freedom to savor. Two weeks to live?—an eternity. Two weeks til school starts?—an eyeblink, a hiccup, a nanosecond. Face the onslaught of relentless whiny pleadings, the weary march of wearier homework excuses, the mindless tittering (remember you can't even say "breast" or "underwear" again)—face all that day after day after day after day and know despair on a first-name hand-holding sacred-decoder-ring basis. Try lunch duty.

But of course! The right stuff!

The first day of my second year of teaching, as I wander the halls with my clipboard in hand, I feel confident. Hall duty is easy today. I chase one or two kids to class, confiscate a hall pass, break up a fight before it gets serious, and, as the period is nearly over, return the clipboard to the office. Then the bell rings, and my education begins: screaming streams of students pour out of classrooms, clogging the hallways (crisis in education? . . . this is a war zone!) elbows dig into my ribs—and they're not mine—nudging insistently, knocking me into a wall of flesh, a behemoth of a boy . . . man (6′11″, 290 pounds of all-state football tackle, who stares down at me menacingly, piggy eyes turning red), whom I recall flunking last year, and I realize, staring up at him, that nobody, no other . . . adult . . . strike that . . . *coach* is anywhere within reach, ready to tear the angry student's hands from around my neck if he chooses to attack. A surge in the stream of students pushes me (thank God!) past the tackle, nearly forcing me to step on a downed freshman (what a neophyte!) groping for his glasses amidst all the trampling feet, while blurs of color rush by: red, fuschia, radioactive green, fluorescent orange, hot pink, black, black, black, drab green—green? . . . my door!—I fight towards it, pushing against the river of students like a spawning salmon trying to get home, squirming, slithering, bobbing up and down, elbowing my way through sweating, jostling bodies, no quarter given and none offered, everybody equalized (what a dangerous thought!), no eddies in which to rest, not even for a moment, only straining . . . straining . . . and . . . I grab at the solid silver door handle, grasp it, grip it—relying on it to help me wrench myself from the bubble-gum infested, wild-eyed, acne-faced river of ensnaring students—wanting only to hug my door. Safety! Home base! At last! I hear a faraway bell: two almost inaudible chimes, which signal the beginning and end of classes. As I grope for my dignity and pull up my socks, a student entering my class asks, "What happened to you?"

Well, say what you will. This is manic, energized, funny writing, vivid in its apparent all-at-onceness, its sense of happening right now, before our eyes. In both imitations the key is the jamming together of detail, the accumulation of the sensory impressions of the experiences, piling up within the sentence, which keeps getting longer and longer—it's a cumulative, of course! (how else could the writer hold so much in tension, relate all these layers?)—and then is interrupted *too* at uneven intervals by parenthetical commentary, sudden asides. The syntax creates suspense: How long can the writer keep this up before the sentence just falls under its own weight? And yet the hotdogging works. The plane comes out of its tail spin, trailing smoke, and streaks over the crowd.

The right stuff.

Push the outside of your own envelopes. Write really long sentences with lots of detail. Ham it up or be serious. Let it fly.

A Note: You can dramatize thought without the manic amplifications of Wolfe, even though these two strategies are related. Just dramatize more calmly, deliberately. Use shorter sentences. The dramatization of thought doesn't even have to give the impression of spontaneity. You can describe a sequence of ideas step by step as they unfolded in the past, as Thomas does in the "Lives of the Cell" paragraph.

STRATEGY THREE: GAPS

*T*his strategy works in the other direction: not expanding and amplifying but cutting, contracting—but cutting and contracting so dramatically that the cutting becomes an envelope-pushing strategy in itself.

What you do here is leave out as much commentary, analysis, explicit interpretation as you possibly can. Cut all the *telling* and leave only the *showing*, the concrete details of scene, character, and story. Stay out of it. "Lie low," as Didion says, and see what develops.

These pictures "shimmer," Didion says. Images and scenes have an aura of meaning that somehow gets communicated without our having to say anything: communicated better, in fact, when we don't say anything. They are vehicles for various suggestive tenors. The principle is metaphorical. Again, when I say my love is a red, red rose, I don't mean that I'm in love with a rose. I've meant a great number of things that I haven't actually said and that I would ruin if I did come out and say.

Prose is not poetry, of course, but in this envelope-pushing strategy you intensify the connotative power of images in just this poetic way. It's a practical strategy, too, a way of tightening up exposition and narrative. You simply don't need as much as you think you do. Readers need the connecting links that worry you as a writer far less than you need them. They spend less time between sentences, jump the gaps easily, lightly. "In narrative, fewest is best," Bernard DeVoto used to say. "If anybody is with you at all, he is probably half a yard ahead of you." Writing just moves faster and more cleanly without excessive explanations. "It shows well enough where it changes," Montaigne understood, "where it concludes, where it begins, where it resumes, without my interlacing it with words, with links and seams introduced for the benefit of weak or heedless ears, and without writing glosses on myself." That's the key. Don't write glosses on yourself.

Didion's prose is the best example of this tight-lipped, sharp-edged approach to description. There are only two or three sentences of explicit interpretation, of telling, in all of "On Going Home," and those are tentative, questioning ("perhaps it is not anymore"). The rest of it is all showing, all shimmering pictures, without Didion's explicitly explaining what the shimmers mean. What does she mean that she and her mother are engaged in a "guerrilla war," that she wants her own daughter to be safe from the "ambushes of family life"? She doesn't say. We understand from the context, have a clear sense of what the metaphors signify. But Didion doesn't *explain* the metaphors. She just uses them. She goes to visit her aunts, who think she is someone else. The baby plays with dust motes in a shaft of sun. That's all. Just that brief description, sketched out, but even without commentary we can see well enough the meaning of the scene, the feelings and ideas it carries: the sad irrelevance of old age, the inability to make connection. She kneels beside her daughter's crib, her face pressed against the slats, and even without her explicitly telling us of her longing and her anxiety for her daughter, we know it and feel it, better than we would if she did come out and tell us. She wants to give her daughter the rivers rising and picnics and the sun, and we know what those details convey, in themselves, as details, what associations they carry: of home, of the past, of tradition, of security, of connection to the land.

You don't need to include thousands and thousands of details. You can choose the key detail, the representative ones, and somehow they carry with them a sense of all the others. Wolfe thinks that there are "status details" in any given scene or for any given character, certain triggering elements of clothing or lighting or personal style that convey through association the whole picture. A writer can invoke a character just by describing his shoes, for example: "Italian suede" or "Nike walkers" or "Birkenstock" conjure up hair style, gestures, age, economic class. A single element of scene can tell the story of all that isn't said:

snow and a crackling fire, a barbecue and a cedar deck. You don't need to say anything more, and it's better if you don't.

You don't even need many of the transitional statements you think you need to go from paragraph to paragraph, sentence to sentence. This seems counterintuitive at first because we've been conditioned to think about logical transition and creating "signposts" to guide readers. That's good advice, too. But it's remarkable how often the writing works logically and reads as coherent when those transitions are eliminated. "Days pass. I see no one," Didion begins a paragraph, simply moving from the last sentence of the previous paragraph, "veterans of a guerrilla war we never understood," changing directions without notifying us in advance. No "furthermore," or "later in that visit," or "as a further example of what I mean." There's a slight bump, but it's a good bump. It gets our attention and we know where we're going anyway. "Everyone says, stay away from ants," Thomas begins a paragraph, without warning, abruptly shifting from beavers and otters. No "to put this another way" or "from another perspective we can see." There's a longer suspension of coherence here, but within a paragraph we're clear about how the ants relate to the theme of the essay as a whole. The suspension has been good, given the essay some tension, tautness.

In a sense writers are often "silent" in their writing, holding back, staying in the background. They let the pictures do the work. It's like looking at a photograph album. A picture here. A picture there. We piece together the history, the narrative. Wolfgang Iser, an influential literary critic, calls this narrative device of silence and concreteness a "gap," and he argues that it's these gaps that draw us as readers into a story. They force us into acts of interpretation, and that's pleasurable, involving. Because we participate in the making of meaning, add our own associations and surmises for each image or piece of dialogue, we experience the story rather than sitting back and hearing it.

Try revising a longer freewriting:

1. Eliminate as many transitional words, phrases, and sentences as possible without sacrificing coherence.

2. Eliminate as much interpretation, commentary, explanation as possible. Some interpretation will necessarily remain, but if there were three sentences before, there should be one now. Consider leaving the thesis implicit or witholding it until the end.

3. Eliminate any passages that don't work for whatever reason, even if they say something you wanted to say.

4. Pull the remaining writing together without additional transitions other than paragraph breaks. Close the spaces.

5. If you need to do additional writing, dramatize rather than explicate; show rather than tell. Consider ending with a scene or portrait rather than a summary interpretation.

Two examples of this kind of revision, the first by Pat.

Original (a freewrite):

I guess the most dramatic change was when I quit my job. I quit in February, in the middle of the year. It was an unusual thing to do, to quit in the middle of the year, but I had had it. I didn't do anything for about 6 months but rest, work in my yard, and rest. It was so nice to rest rest rest. I had been tired, stressed. I seemed to look at the fir trees across the field forever. The dogwood blossoms came and went. My apples grew and ripened and I rested.

After 2 or 3 months I began to be at peace with myself. I began to be settled into nature. The true way humans should be. Nestled in nature, at rest, in peace.

Little by little I began to do more. I did a little part time work, and I worked at odd jobs, but I have never let myself get stressed as I had. I'm more important than that. The human race deserves more than the merry-go-round stress machine that it is on. We have to take care of ourselves. We need to be centered in our being so that nothing is as important as ourselves.

So the change was from frantic to calm. From stress to quiet, still. From war to peace.

I can feel it inside still, the calming, calming and quieting of the soul into its surroundings, the becoming part of the earth, eternal, maternal, ever quiet.

Now it is spring and the apple blossom petals are falling on my shoulders.

Revision:

I didn't do anything for about six months. I rested. I worked in my yard and rested. I seemed to look at the fir trees across the field forever. The dogwood blossoms came and went. My apples grew from buds and ripened, and I rested.

After two or three months I began to be at peace with myself. I began to be settled in nature. Nestled in nature. At rest.

Little by little I began to do more. I did odd jobs, never enough to let myself get stressed, taking care of myself, being centered in my being, nothing as important as myself, no one taking care of me as well as I can.

I went from frantic to calm, noise to quiet, from war to peace.

Now it is spring again, and the apple blossom petals fall on my shoulders.

More is involved in the creation of gaps than simple economizing, simple cutting of wordiness—what we talked about in Chapter 3. Information and ideas get cut here—the fact that Pat quit her job, for example. What also gets eliminated is the corny commentary and interpretation of the freewriting. Corniness is inevitable for part of the freewriting as Pat thinks aloud about her feelings and experiences, moving past the first superficial layer to the concreteness and images underneath, the fir trees and the apple blossoms. The revision is calmer, quieter, centered. Behind and through the concrete imagery Pat can convey the feeling of the original clichés without indulging in them.

Now here's Debra.

Original:

After all the encouragement and support from my husband, I began to realize that I was really and truly going back to school. I was nervous and excited. I had the normal worries about whether or not I would fit in and be accepted among students a few years younger than me. I was also very excited and even took great joy in paying $34.95 for my first textbook.

I am now working on my second term since coming back to school. I feel very challenged and a lot more satisfied with my life and with the direction it is going. My brain is finally getting the workout it needed for me to feel good about myself. My decision to come back to school was not an easy one and it has required myself and my husband to make a few personal sacrifices, but for what school has already given me in the way I feel about myself it is worth all the sacrifices we've made.

Revision:

I walked into the bookstore trying to look like any other college girl. I tried to mask my excitement but felt great joy paying $34.95 for my first textbook. My next stop was the library. I proudly handed the man behind the front desk my I.D. card and in return I carried Blake's *Songs of Innocence and Experience* home with me.

Four pages and three tests are on my agenda for the next week. I've got to remember why the moon has a dark side, I need to read Elbow's section on "voice" again. I need to study the imperative forms of French verbs. My husband waves as he hurries out the door for work at job number two. I munch on my fourth peanut butter sandwich of the week. I feel wonderful.

This revision, too, is more than a simple cutting. It's a radical reseeing of the subject, everything dramatized, brought alive through detail. There is some statement of feeling in the revision—"great joy," "I feel wonderful"—but these are earned by the images of carrying away Blake and munching sandwiches. We experience Debra's feeling of excitement in the second version rather than simply being told about it.

GAPS CONTINUED: THE COLLAGE

*T*he collage form takes the notion of gaps still further, expanding paragraph indentations into blank spaces between sections, eliminating all transition, arranging chunks of language of various sizes in imagistic, qualitative, alternating patterns of movement. Write about a given subject from different angles—descriptive, narrative, analytical, personal, objective—not sure of where you're going yet or even what your central purpose is yet. Just write. Pile up the pieces of writing. Then: find the best places, literally cut them away from their surroundings, and arrange them all on a table, a bed, the floor. What should come first? What groupings seem to make sense? What sequence? What meaning or center comes out of this collection of strong or workable writing?

Use blank space to indicate the movement from one grouping to the next. Make some groupings several paragraphs long; others shorter; others just a short sentence or two. Create spatial variety. Use single spacing, indentation, italics, parentheses, underlining—any visual, graphic device—to indicate the variety of pieces.

The collage form has become popular in contemporary prose. Didion's famous essay "Slouching Towards Bethlehem" is a collection of pieces, for example, clustered around a central theme, the effort to report the counterculture of Haight Ashbury. Thomas's "Lives of a Cell," is a collage, too, the word "item" rather than blank space indicating the progression, the leaping of the gaps. Many of John McPhee's *New Yorker* pieces are collagelike, although the pieces are often long, the gaps few and far between. Most of Annie Dillard's work is structured as collage—for example, her autobiography, *An American Childhood*. The device is common in much fiction, to varying degrees.

A collage essay of my own:

On Screens

> I live in the World rather as a Spectator of Mankind, than as one of the species. . . . I have acted in all the Parts of my Life as a looker-on.
> —Joseph Addison, *The Spectator*

In the spring I took my five year old daughter camping on the Oregon Coast. It was still cold, and Maggie wore a pink stocking cap over her forehead, folded up, like a flapper. She giggled at me as we walked or clowned in the sand.

It was one of those times when everything seemed to be in equilibrium. There was a balance. The sun was going down and a windsurfer worked back and forth in the waves, leaning out perpendicular to the board, bouncing on the crests, collapsing at the end of the run and swimming back out to start over. I was admiring his skill. I was glad to be seeing him, glad to be *seeing*. The satisfaction I felt was precisely in the watching, and for a moment—this was the surprise, like a surge of recognition, of happiness almost—for a moment that act of watching seemed acceptable, not a failure to act, an absence of skill, but a subtle act, a subtle skill itself. Watching, looking on, I rode the crest of his expert motions, my mind like a sail, filling with the pearl-gray light.

My son is less patient with my epiphanies. We went camping on Mary's Peak the following weekend, the highest point in the Coast Range, and from the beginning he was pushing and pestering and knocking things over, chattering away about soccer and the playground and the triumphs of first grade, always in motion. He wanted to fly fish. He wanted to bow hunt. He wanted to build a lean-to out of cedar boughs.

What I wanted was time. I had images of sitting around the fire telling stories and watching the moon rise. And we did that later, and John listened, squirming in the camp chair, falling over once or twice. The moon was huge coming up over the fir trees, and sudden, unexpected. At twilight we heard the rinsing, falling sound of the wood thrush, and John said, "He keeps repeating himself, doesn't he, Dad, saying the same thing over and over." Later the stars silenced him, silenced us both.

But the next day on our hike John was grabbing sticks and interrogating each marmot hole. Stumps were dragons and branches uzzis. He wanted to whack all the trees and flush out all the animals, and his metaphors were all of machinery—jets, tanks, chain saws. He would race up the trail, tear off into the ferns, then slouch down on a log and complain about how tired his feet were. A lot of this energy comes from simple boyishness, of course. It's physiological. But there's a difference in temperament between my son and me, too. John is a person of his hands, and I am a person of my eyes. He wants to build and make and take apart. I want to look, understand, reflect. My relationship with him reproduces my relationship with my father, who was also a person of his hands, an electrician and mechanic, barrel-chested and strong. I remember Dad wrestling a piano down the stairs once when I let go of the other end, or inspecting the '56 Chevy I wanted to buy, leaning over the engine and squinting at the fuel pump.

Now I find myself walking up a trail with this wonderful little boy who wants nothing more than to sail boats and learn knots and build go-carts. What he wants is the lore of the old pre-ecology, slash-and-burn Boy Scout Handbook. The pressure on me is to fit the Boy Scout image of father, father as Scoutmaster, father as initiator into masculine expertise: showing his son how to clean a shotgun or gut a pheasant or build model airplanes with real motors. And they're standing together on the brow of a hill, the man and his son, and the man is leaning over, pointing at something off in the distance, and the boy is looking, smiling, his hair slicked back, and they're both wearing red plaid hunting jackets.

In my dream Maggie is caught in a transporter beam arcing between the microwave and the VCR. There's an odd plausibility about it, since the VCR in the playroom and the microwave in the kitchen are positioned at such an angle that someone could get caught in a crossfire. It's like the suddenness of an accident with electricity. Maggie is sitting in front of the VCR watching a tape and when I turn on the microwave a sharp blue light shoots out, some terrible circuit is completed, and suddenly Maggie disappears, like Jean-Luc Picard in the transporter. I run into the playroom, stop the VCR, hold my breath, and start rewinding, slowly, calibrating the exact moment Maggie will reappear. Somehow I know that she has been absorbed into the tape, literally made into film, and that it is only by playing back the VCR to the exact moment of her disappearance that I can claim her again. I reach the right place on the tape, press "play," my hands shaking, and when she reappears, her image sparkling in the air, I start grabbing for her, pulling at the static charges, the shimmering. But there is nothing solid to hold onto, nothing there, except a large blue notebook cradled in her arms, a three ring binder thick with paper. Time is passing. Hold on to the notebook! I shout. Don't let go! But then I pull, Maggie releases her arms, the image breaks up, and I fall back on the floor, the notebook in my hands. Maggie is gone.

Freud thought dreams were a kind of screen to block out the horror and complexity of the unconscious mind. Or the mind was a screener, filtering out and transforming this energy into something manageable. Character depends on "screens against full consciousness," Ernest Becker says in an analysis of Freud, "screens for terror," "screens against despair." It's not hard to read my dream of screens. A father's longing for a daughter growing up. Uneasiness about the world taking her away—just "the world," the world of grown-ups and challenges that has always been there, but also the "modern world," the world of technology, the world of computers and devices and the greenhouse effect, global warming.

Writing the dream down now I screen and filter it, try to find what's valuable in it. Make a pattern of it.

I go to the shore to find the pattern. I take my daughter there when I dream of her disappearing. The sound of the waves drowns out our other voices. I take my son to the mountain when I feel him slipping away, when he seems blurred and indistinct. There is a stand of noble fir near the summit, hundreds of years old, and the forest beneath them is deep and dark and shot through with light.

The Kalapuya Indians called Mary's Peak Tch Tee Man Wi, or spirit mountain. It was the place they went for vision quests, fasting and praying and chanting in the open meadows, their hands upraised. I went to Tch Tee Man Wi on a quest for vision, too, though only for the weekend, car camping. I went to the mountain to see what I could see: the cathedral floor of ferns and rotting logs, the sweep of the valley, the lupin and daisies.

Vision quests are problematic now, of course. We have to take them ironically, cautiously. Maggie and I camped in a playground along the coast highway as crowded as an apartment house, listening all night to the RVs whizzing down the coast, walking along a creek the next day cluttered with plastic wrappers and Coke cans. From the top of Mary's Peak John and I could hardly see the valley through the haze of smoke, and looking west toward the ocean we could see square on square of clearcutting.

Or maybe beauty and truth are illusory to begin with, a kind of mental haze, the product of imaginative industry, obscuring our view of the actual landscape. Maybe there is nothing but whirring atoms in space, brute extension in time, value only the projection of the mind.

Dorothy and the Scarecrow and the Tin Man and the Cowardly Lion are all standing before the terrible Oz. The Lion roars, frightening Toto, who tips over the "screen" standing in the corner of the great hall. The next moment the group is filled with wonder. For "there they saw, standing in just the spot the screen had hidden, a little, old man, with a bald head and wrinkled face, who seemed to be as much surprised as they were." There is no magic in Oz, only an ordinary man with a bag of tricks. Maybe in the postmodern version of the story there would be a machine behind the screen, no man at all—a word processor, serated pages pouring out of a printer.

I am thinking still of the spring, of Maggie and me sitting in the dune grass in the evening watching the windsurfer.

Someone was flying a kite, too, and it occurred to me that watchers, seers, lookers-on are like kite-flyers, the line of their vision like a string, and that the act of seeing, of watching, if it is intense enough, concentrated enough, can almost manipulate the thing seen, move it, make it dance, like the kite flyer manipulating the kite, keeping it aloft.

Maggie started drawing pictures that evening, and later we put them in a little book describing our trip. She dictated the captions: "We saw jellyfish and we smashed the round seaweed floats. We walked really far." "This is us walking on the beach." "This is the surf-boarder and the sea."

I am remembering John and I sitting with our backs against the wall of the weather station at the summit, the wind blowing hard across the meadow grass, and the clouds racing up at us from the valley below. They formed and reformed around us, and behind them were banks and banks of other clouds, cirrus and cumulus and stratus, like a festival of clouds, like Spielberg clouds, boiling and moving in time-lapse photography. We thought of other metaphors: a floating herd of cows, a race of balloons, some strange aliens. There was an odd illusion of intelligence about them, as if they were pausing somehow to look us over—like porpoises swimming in the air.

Sitting there with our backs against the weather station, the clearcutting hidden by the clouds below us, it wasn't hard to imagine the Kalapuya fasting and praying on the summit and the wraiths of clouds forming and reforming before them. It wasn't hard, for a moment, to imagine ourselves in the presence of God, in the presence of something.

Writing this down now I screen and filter memory, find a pattern in it. The screen glows and the trees move in the wind. The screen is a sieve, a riddle. It is blind. It is a covered frame and within it there are green lines of words like a mesh of light. The light is yarn and the screen a loom and the cursor like a shuttle moving in and out of the threads, in and out.

There are five pieces here, two descriptive pieces on either end of a "thesis" piece, a more explicit reflection on the meaning of the scenes I describe. But I want the implications of "screen" to emerge finally from the scenes themselves: screen as in veil, cloud, filter; screen as in watching, hiding, creatively interpreting and patterning experience. I don't have a thesis in the sense of some definitive conclusion. What I have is the experience and the questioning itself, the collage form also allowing me to dramatize the process of my thinking (combining the first and third strategies here).

COMPROMISE AND SUBVERSION

*M*ost of the time, of course, you have to be more explicit and less exploratory, state transitions and take out parentheses. Most of the time you have to be more beige. Classes don't usually allow collages for term papers or dramatizations of thought for essay exams.

Use the free/style in those situations—free/style in the original sense of a method for getting words down on the page quickly and easily, writing simply, naturally. If free/style is a machine you can turn up high for amplification and envelope pushing, it's also a machine you can turn down low to get the day-to-day work done efficiently and with less pain.

Pushing language to these limits of amplification or compression is good, then, just for the exercise, good for what it tells you about what language can do. Returning from those edges, you have more power as a stylist than you had before, more options to incorporate in your ordinary, workaday prose, to sneak into your memos and reports. You just kind of keep them quiet.

And yet. And yet.

There's that old joke about a man on his hands and knees underneath a lamp post. Another man comes up and asks: Whatcha looking for?

My watch.

Where'd you lose it?

Over there (pointing to a dark piece of ground by the bushes).

So why are you looking for it over here?

The light's better.

Sometimes we hold to ideas simply because they're easy to hold, not because they're true, or should be true. Sometimes it's not a bad thing to maintain a quiet resistance.

In a journal entry made in 1854, when he was thirty-six, on the verge of publishing *Walden*, Thoreau describes reading a scientific report:

> I look over the report of the doings of a scientific association and am surprised that there is so little life to be reported; I am put off with a parcel of dry technical terms. Anything living is easily and naturally expressed in popular language. I cannot help suspecting that the life of these learned professors has been almost as inhuman and wooden as a rain-gauge or self-registering magnetic machine. They communicate no fact which rises to the temperature of blood-heat. It doesn't all amount to one rhyme.

Like Thoreau, the free/style insists that "anything living is easily and naturally expressed in popular language"; insists that life be reported, that the temperature of prose be raised to blood-heat. "There is no such thing as pure *objective* observation," Thoreau says earlier in this entry. "The sum of what the writer of whatever class has to report is simply some human experience, whether he be poet or philosopher or man of science."

Free/style, too, though it will settle for less, hopes for the reporting of a human experience, the account of a real person in a real place and time. And behind that hope is a belief in the value of experience, the dignity of the person.

SKETCHBOOK

A FINAL SUGGESTION FOR WRITING

In this chapter I've included several suggestions along the way for revising the practice pieces or other new pieces of writing.

As another option, a good way of concluding your first experience with the free/style: write a collage essay reflecting on an important issue, problem, theme, in your own life.

Freewrite in and around the theme, first from this angle, now from that. Be concrete. Concentrate on recreating each experience or piece of experience in as much detail as you can without worrying at this stage about how the pieces add up.

Do freewrites dramatizing your thinking now and then; others stylistically pushing the outside of the envelope; others describing a significant scene or event without explicitly explaining its meaning.

When you've piled up enough pieces from enough angles, spread them all out and see what order they go in, using blank space to separate the major parts.

A possible topic:

A Writing Life: a reflection on your experience as a writer, past and present. Questions to consider: What have been your successes and failures as a writer? (Use whatever parts of the first practice piece you find useful here.) Who have your readers been and how have they motivated or discouraged you? Where and when do you write? What has been the process in the past, and the process now? Do you write anything you never show anyone? What kind of writing do you enjoy doing? Is there a kind you would prefer doing that you don't have a chance to do now? Why is writing worth all the trouble? Is there a conflict between your private and public self as a writer, between what you want to say and what you have to say? Does there need to be? Does the free/style make sense in your experience as a writer?

·····································

INDEX

ABS, *see* Absolute
Absolute (ABS), in cumulative sentences, 119, 120, 125–127, 130
Abstract jargon, defense of, 55–56
AC, *see* Adjective clusters
Academic writing, 133–136
Accident, in free/style, 38
Adding, in COAPing, 12, 13, 23
Adjective clusters (AC)
   in cumulative sentences, 120, 121, 122, 124–125, 127
   emphatic, 148
Allen, Woody, 160
Alliteration, 65
American Childhood, An (Dillard), 182
Amplification, of sentences, 172–176
Analyzing (A)
   in essays, 95–96, 97, 98, 101–104
   in paragraphs, 90, 92, 93, 101, 102, 103, 104
"And," sentence beginning with, 159
Anne (student writer), 59–61, 64, 69–70, 71
Antimetabole, 160
Aristotle, 29
"Artful artlessness," 37–38
Assonance, 64
Asyndeton, in cumulative sentences, 152–153
Audience, paradox of, 7–8
Authenticity, *see* Simplicity

Bacon, Francis, 123, 161
Balance, in sentence, 160
Baldwin, James, 36, 123

Barzun, Jacques, 30
Bean, John, 135
Berry, Wendell, 36
Blocs, paragraphs as, 85
Braddock, Richard, 85–86
Brunson, Mark, 53, 55
Burke, Kenneth, 56, 99–100

Capote, Truman, 128
Carver, Raymond, 27
Cicero, 29
COAPing, 40, 73
   for academic writing, 134
   for longer projects, 24
   for revision, 11–24
Collage, 165, 181–188
Colon, in cumulative sentences, 150–151
Comma, cumulative sentence and, 141–142
Comma splices, 142, 143–144
Comparison, at beginning of sentence, 160
Compound sentence, 158–159
   cumulatives as part of, 141
Concluding
   in essays, 96, 98
   in paragraphs, 90, 92, 94, 102
Concreteness
   in diction, 56–58
   in paragraphs, 100–104
Connotation, of words, 72
Consonance, 65, 66
Content, form and, 78, 104–105; *see also* Paragraphing
Contrast, in sentences, 162